AN UNOFFICIAL GUIDE TO
BATTLE ROYALE

BATTLE PASS SUCCESS FOR FORTNITERS

MASTER COMBAT BOOK #6

JASON R. RICH

Sky Pony Press
New York

Sky Pony Press books may be purchased in bulk at special discounts for sales promotion, corporate gifts, fund-raising, or educational purposes. Special editions can also be created to specifications. For details, contact the Special Sales Department, Sky Pony Press, 307 West 36th Street, 11th Floor, New York, NY 10018 or info@skyhorsepublishing.com.

Sky Pony® is a registered trademark of Skyhorse Publishing, Inc.®, a Delaware corporation.

Visit our website at www.skyhorsepublishing.com.

10 9 8 7 6 5 4 3 2 1

Library of Congress Cataloging-in-Publication Data is available on file.

Cover design by Brian Peterson
Cover artwork by Getty Images Interior photography by Jason R. Rich

Print ISBN: 978-1-5107-5706-6
E-Book ISBN: 978-1-5107-5717-2

Printed in the United States of America

TABLE OF CONTENTS

SECTION 1

FORTNITE: BATTLE ROYALE
OVERVIEW

Since Epic Games initially launched *Fortnite* back in July 2017, the game has evolved a lot, and it has truly become a worldwide gaming phenomenon! Despite all of the changes continuously being made to *Fortnite: Battle Royale*, each exciting match continues to focus on battle royale–style combat, arsenal management, building, survival, and exploration.

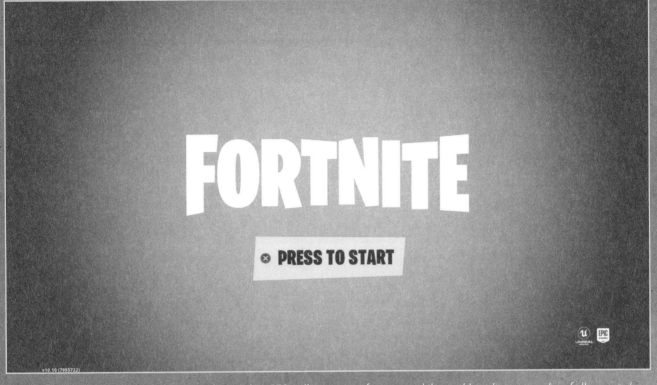

Fortnite: Battle Royale has already attracted more than 250 million gamers from around the world, and more people–of all ages and gaming skill levels–begin playing Fortnite for the first time each and every day!

The first portion of this unofficial guide offers a comprehensive overview of *Fortnite* and *Fortnite: Battle Royale*. This information will help you become a better player and prepare you to successfully complete **Missions** and **Challenges**.

The second part of this guide focuses specifically on seasonal **Battle Passes** and how to acquire **Battle Stars** to unlock **Battle Pass Tiers** to earn **Rewards**. You'll also discover how to complete other Missions and Challenges offered in the game.

Keep in mind, while this guide was written during Season 10 of *Fortnite: Battle Royale*, all of the information and strategies you'll discover apply to *all* gaming seasons, including the current one.

Many Different Gaming Experiences Are Available

Fortnite *currently includes three unique gaming experiences—* Fortnite: Battle Royale, Fortnite: Creative, *and* Fortnite: Save the World. *Each put your gaming skills to the ultimate test in a slightly different way.*

By the end of each match, only one soldier will remain alive and achieve #1 Victory Royale. What ultimately happens during each match, however, depends a lot on the actions of the gamers participating, as well as the expansion and movement of the deadly storm. As a result, every match is different.

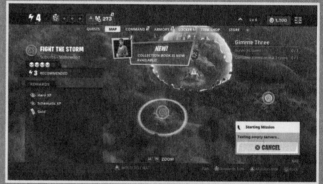

Fortnite: Battle Royale's **Solo** *game play mode, for example, offers an online-based, multi-player, battle royale-style gaming experience. Each player controls one soldier. At the start of each match, 100 soldiers (each controlled by a different gamer in real time) are transported to the mysterious island.*

Fortnite: Save the World *offers a story-based challenge. Players must defeat computer-controlled adversaries and accomplish challenges and obstacles in order to proceed through the game. Unlike* Fortnite: Battle Royale, *which can be downloaded and played for free, at least for now,* Save the World *must be purchased and downloaded, and is not currently available for play on smartphones or tablets.*

For those who want to create their own island and then establish the rules of engagement for the combat that takes place during a match, there's Fortnite: Creative. This version of Fortnite allows gamers to share the unique islands and matches they design from scratch, plus develop different types of gaming experiences that don't necessarily focus on combat.

Prepare Yourself for Many Intense *Fortnite: Battle Royale* Matches

In addition to the **Solo** game play mode in *Fortnite: Battle Royale*, this version of the game includes the **Duos**, **Squads**, and **Playground** modes, along with an ever-changing selection of temporary gaming modes.

The limited-time game play modes often include "Team Rumbles" that involve 100 gamers being divided up into two or three teams. The first team to accomplish a specific goal wins the match. The required objectives for Team Rumble and Arena-style matches change regularly and vary greatly.

In **Solo** game play mode, you'll encounter 99 other soldiers on the island at the start of every match. Each soldier is controlled in real time by a different gamer. As you engage in combat, gather resources, build, and manage your own soldier's arsenal of weapons, for example, you'll also need to contend with the deadly storm that forms on the island.

As the storm slowly expands and moves, it makes more and more of the island uninhabitable. During the final minutes of a match (referred to as the End Game), only a few soldiers remain alive, and almost the entire island is rendered uninhabitable by the storm. To become the last remaining soldier on the island, you'll be forced into combat. The areas displayed on the Island Map in pink have already been ravaged by the storm. Stay out of these potentially lethal areas whenever possible!

When you opt to experience *Fortnite: Battle Royale*'s **Duos** game play mode, you'll be able to team up with one other gamer—either a random person or one of your online friends—as you face challenges from up to 98 other gamers who you'll encounter on the island during the match.

Fortnite: Battle Royale's **Squads** game play mode allows your soldier to join a four-person squad. During a Squads match, a total of 25 four-soldier squads compete against each other. Your squad can include yourself and three strangers (selected by the game), or you're able to choose your squad mates by inviting online friends to join your Party (or by accepting invites from your online friends).

On the Lobby screen, when you see yellow banners surrounding your soldier that say, "[Username] Invited You!," these are invitations received from other gamers. Shown here, an invite is displayed to the left of the soldier (they're displayed in the center of the screen). Also, whenever there's an important announcement from Epic Games that impacts game play, a notice is displayed near the bottom-center of the Lobby screen.

Each match ends when there's only one soldier, a two-soldier team, or at least one member of a squad remaining alive on the island—everyone else must be defeated! To become an accomplished *Fortnite: Battle Royale* player, you'll need to master a wide range of skills and continuously juggle multiple responsibilities during each match.

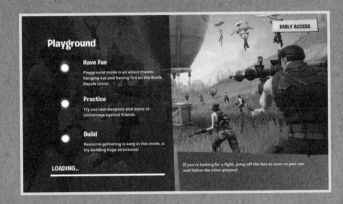

Playground *mode allows your soldier to visit and explore the island alone or with friends, and practice using the weapons, vehicles, tools, and resources available, without having to worry about being eliminated from a match. Soldiers respawn almost instantly in Playground mode, plus it's possible to customize the rules of engagement if you're visiting the island with other gamers.*

Playground mode is the perfect place to practice and improve your gaming skills, while having plenty of freedom to explore each of the unique points of interest (locations) that are featured within the island during any gaming season. While in Playground mode, you cannot earn Experience Points (XP) or complete Missions or Challenges related to Battle Passes, Missions, Events, Styles, or Free Pass Challenges.

Develop Your Muscle Memory

If you're playing *Fortnite: Battle Royale* on a computer, chances are you'll control the game using your computer's keyboard and mouse. Every action and command in the game requires you to quickly press specific keyboard key and/or mouse button combinations to achieve success.

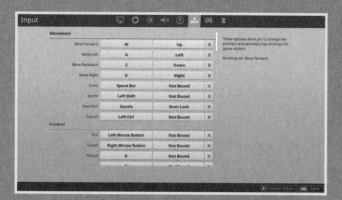

From the Input submenu within Settings (when using a keyboard and mouse to control the game), you're able to customize the key bindings associated with Fortnite: Battle Royale.

Some computer gamers opt to connect a gaming controller to their computer, which is what most players use to control the action when experiencing *Fortnite* on a PlayStation 4, Xbox One, or Nintendo Switch, for example.

There are several different controller layouts available from the Controller submenu within Settings. Regardless of which controller layout you choose, learn how to perform all of the actions, moves, and commands required during a match. Shown here is the Input submenu within Settings on a Windows PC.

This is the Controller submenu within Settings shown on a PS4.

Since many gamers believe that using a keyboard and mouse offers more precise control over the Fortnite gaming experience than using a controller, most console-based gaming systems, including the PS4 and Xbox One, allow for an optional computer keyboard and mouse to be connected. Shown here is the optional Razer Turret keyboard and mouse for the Xbox One that's available from Razer ($249.99, www.razer.com/gaming-keyboards-keypads/razer-turret-for-xbox-one).

There are specialized keyboards, mice, controllers, and gaming headsets designed to improve your reaction time and precision when playing games like *Fortnite: Battle Royale.* At some point, you may discover that upgrading your gaming gear will help you achieve more success when competing against highly skilled and experienced players.

For help connecting a USB keyboard and mouse to your Xbox One, for example, check out this page of Microsoft's website—https://support.xbox.com/en-US/xbox-one/ease-of-access/mouse-keyboard. Similar information for PS4 gamers can be found here: https://support.playstation.com/s/article/Use-Keyboard-and-Mouse-with-PS4.

No matter how you opt to control the action in *Fortnite*, it's absolutely essential that you memorize the controller buttons or keyboard/mouse keys needed to perform every task, function, and action required. Then, once you've memorized the controls, practice using them, so that you develop your *muscle memory* specifically for *Fortnite*.

Once your muscle memory has been honed, you won't need to waste valuable time thinking about what button or key to press to achieve specific tasks or objectives. This allows you to vastly improve your reaction time when it comes to aiming and using weapons, building, moving around, replenishing your soldier's Health and Shields, launching attacks, or retreating from dangerous situations.

Quick reaction time is essential when playing *Fortnite: Battle Royale.* Even a fraction of a second delay could result in your soldier's ultimate demise. Thus, in addition to developing your muscle memory for the game, you'll want to experience *Fortnite* using the fastest Internet connection possible.

To improve their gaming experience, pro gamers also often opt to tweak the controller or keyboard/mouse sensitivity options from the Settings submenus.

A Soldier Has Several Core Responsibilities During Each Match

During each match, you'll have six core responsibilities. You'll often need to manage several of these responsibilities at the same time, while continuously analyzing the situation you're in. The ability to make quick decisions that will impact your chances of survival, and then appropriately reacting to whatever is happening around you (by taking advantage of the weapons, tools, transportation options, and resources at your disposal) is a key gaming skill.

Knowing what to expect during each match isn't enough. What will allow you to become an awesome *Fortnite: Battle Royale* gamer and achieve #1 Victory Royale is practice . . . a lot of practice!

Responsibility #1—Find, Build, and Manage Your Arsenal

When your soldier first lands on the island at the start of each match they'll be armed only with their trusty Harvesting Tool. While this can be used as a close-range weapon, it's better suited for collecting (harvesting) wood, stone, and metal, which are the resources used for building on the island.

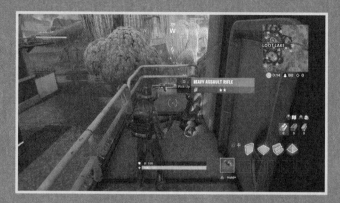

In order to defeat your adversaries, you'll need to find and grab weapons, and ensure you always have an ample supply of the proper ammunition on hand to use the weapons at your disposal. Shown here, an Uncommon-ranked Heavy Assault Rifle was spotted and picked up within moments after the soldier landed on the island at the start of a match. Any type of Assault Rifle is considered a versatile weapon because it works well at close or mid-range. Its accuracy decreases the farther you are from the target, however.

At any given time, more than 100 types of weapons can be found and collected on the island. Epic Games continuously releases new weapons into the game, and at the same time, vaults or tweaks existing weapons, so the assortment of available weapons is always changing.

Each weapon can be categorized by its type—such as a Handgun (Pistol), Shotgun, Assault Rifle (AR), Submachine Gun (SMG), Minigun, Sniper Rifle, or Rocket Launcher. There's also an ever-changing assortment of throwable and explosive weapons at your soldier's disposal.

As you'll discover, multiple types of weapons within each weapon category are offered. For example, Pistols, Hand Canons, Six Shooters, Suppressed Pistols, Duel Pistols, and Revolvers all fall into the handgun category. A basic grey (Common-ranked) Pistol is shown here. This is a close-range weapon that's considered by most as the weakest weapon in the game. If you're consistently able to win firefights using just a grey Pistol, you can consider yourself to be a highly skilled gamer!

Learn About *Fortnite*'s Weapon Categories

Close-Range Weapons—Any type of handgun (such as a Pistol) is an example of a close-range weapon. These are best used when you're fighting within a structure and you're not too far away from your target. As you get farther away from your target, the weapon will become harder to aim and inflict less damage. Pistols tend to be the weakest guns in the game. When you have the opportunity to switch them out for more powerful and versatile close- to mid-range weapons, do so. Shown here is a purple, Epic-ranked Suppressed Pistol. It's just one example of a close-range weapon.

Mid-Range Weapons–These tend to be more versatile than close-range weapons, so they can be used with decent accuracy in a broader range of indoor or outdoor combat scenarios. Shown here are the stats from a soldier's inventory screen for an orange, Legendary-ranked Tactical Shotgun. While Legendary weapons are rare, a Tactical Shotgun is one of many mid-range weapons you're likely to find on the island during a match, although the available weapon selection on the island changes regularly.

When a Bolt-Action Sniper Rifle (or any type of weapon with a scope) is active, press the Aim button to switch to this scope view. It allows you to zoom in on your target and achieve extremely precise aim from a great distance.

Long-Range Weapons–Sniper Rifles with a scope are just one example of a long-range weapon that shoots bullets with extreme accuracy when you're far away from your target. Using any weapon with a scope, if you just point the gun and shoot, you'll experience less accuracy than if you first press the Aim button, position your enemy within the targeting crosshairs, and then fire the gun. A blue, Rare-ranked Bolt-Action Sniper Rifle (shown here) is an example of a long-range weapon that has a built-in scope.

Explosive Weapons–As you explore the island, you'll be able to find, grab, store, and then use a variety of different throwable explosive weapons, such as Grenades and Stink Bombs (shown here). These tend to work best when you're mid-range from your opponent, since you don't want your soldier to be too close to the explosion that occurs once any of these weapons detonate.

Once tossed, a Stink Bomb generates a cloud of toxic smoke for about 9 seconds. For every half-second a soldier gets caught in the poisonous cloud, they receive 5 HP damage. It's best to use this weapon in a confined space, so it takes longer for enemies to escape the blast.

Grenades (shown here) are a popular explosive weapon that can be tossed at a target. Like many throwable explosive weapons, if you throw one at a solid object, such as the wall of a building, it will bounce off of it. You're better off tossing an explosive weapon through an open window or the door of a building, house, or structure, or throwing it close to an enemy so that they get caught in the blast zone.

Many of the throwable explosive weapons featured in Fortnite: Battle Royale *take a few seconds to detonate after being thrown. Be sure to take this delay into account when planning your attacks. Each weapon in this category has a different detonation delay. When a throwable explosive weapon is active, as your soldier is aiming it, you'll see a blue aiming arch that'll help you throw the weapon at a perfect angle. Shown here, the goal was to toss a Grenade through the second story's open window.*

The aiming process for throwable weapons is different than shooting a gun. Notice the targeting crosshairs look different. When you toss a Grenade, it follows an arc-like trajectory. As you're aiming the Grenade, you'll see an outline for the trajectory for that weapon. In some cases, if you're trying to toss a Grenade through a small open window of a building or fortress,

it may be necessary to aim slightly higher than your intended target. Upon detonation, a throwable weapon typically explodes. This can cause damage to or the destruction of a building or structure, and/or inflict harm on enemy soldiers.

Explosive Projectile Weapons Launchers— Anytime you need to destroy buildings, structures, fortresses, or vehicles, for example, as well as the enemies within them, projectile explosive weapons allow you to aim from a distance, and then shoot explosive ammo with extreme accuracy toward your target.

Some of the Projectile Explosive Weapons you may discover on the island include: Rocket Launchers, Guided Missile Launchers, Grenade Launchers, Boom Bows, and/or Quad Launchers. Depending on the gaming season, not all of these weapons will be available all of the time.

A Grenade Launcher allows you to shoot Grenades a lot farther than a handheld Grenade can be thrown. Whether they're shot or thrown, Grenades function the same way. It's best to shoot or toss them through an open door or window so they land inside of a structure before they detonate in order to cause destructive damage to a structure. If a Grenade hits a solid wall, it will bounce off of it.

Traps and Specialty Weapons–During each gaming season, a different selection of Traps and specialty weapons are made available. A Trap, for example, can be placed on any flat surface, such as a floor, ceiling, or wall of a structure. Depending on the type of Trap being used, an enemy that gets caught in one could be instantly defeated or at least injured. In some cases, Traps have a different impact on the soldier who activates it.

Shown here are the stats for an Uncommon Heavy Assault Rifle. You can see this information by selecting a weapon in your soldier's inventory and then viewing this inventory screen (when it's safe to do so during a match).

Traps get stored in your soldier's inventory with their ammo and resources, so they do not require an inventory slot. Thus, you can carry as many Traps as you can find and collect, and then use them at your discretion. When placing a Trap, it's best to position it in a place where your enemy won't see it—until it's too late—so be creative when setting them.

Each Type of Weapon Has Different Capabilities

There are several different model handguns typically available on the island. Some types of handguns have higher Damage and DPS ratings, a faster Fire Rate, a larger Magazine Size, and/or faster Reload time than others. The most versatile type of handgun is a Scoped Revolver. Thanks to its scope, it can be used from any distance. Ideally, you want to find and keep a Legendary Scoped Revolver in your arsenal.

Shotguns are also versatile weapons, since they can cause damage from almost any distance. The trick is to find and grab the best ranked and most powerful Shotgun model you can during a match. Shotguns fire Shells, which burst apart when fired, meaning each shot can inflict damage over a greater area, based on the distance a round travels before impact. When the distance is too far, the Shell fragments disburse over a greater area. This reduces the damage each piece of Shell shrapnel causes on its target.

Assault Rifles (ARs) are the most versatile weapons, because they're powerful and useful at close range or mid-range.

Shown here is a blue, Rare-ranked Pump Shotgun, which is typically one of the more common weapons you'll find on the island. This type of weapon works nicely as a close-range weapon when you're exploring the inside of houses, buildings, or structures, for example. It also has rather accurate mid-range aiming capabilities.

The drawback to Shotguns is they typically have a small Magazine (Mag) Size, capable of holding just one or two Shells at a time before a Reload is needed. These weapons also tend to have a slow Reload Time. For example, a Legendary Double Barrel Shotgun takes 2.7 seconds to reload.

Sniper Rifles are powerful long-range weapons that include a scope. They tend to have a small Magazine size and long Reload time, but they're great for achieving headshots from a distance, especially if you catch your enemy off-guard and standing still. The different types of Sniper Rifles are best used during the early- to mid-stages of a match, when enemies can still be far apart. During the End Game, all remaining soldiers are typically very close together, so a Sniper Rifle is often less useful.

Try to find and use a Sniper Rifle with a large Magazine (Mag) Size, so you'll need to reload less frequently during firefights. When using a weapon with a small Mag Size, position your soldier behind a protective barrier when reloading.

One benefit to a Legendary Suppressed Sniper Rifle, for example, is that it makes very little noise when fired. This makes it harder for your target(s) to pinpoint your location when they're far away. If your enemy can't figure out where your soldier is, they can't accurately shoot back.

Submachine Guns (SMGs) are excellent at close- to mid-range, because they have a very fast Fire Rate and can cause a good amount of damage quickly. Their Magazine (Mag) Size tends to be rather large (20 rounds or more before a Reload is required). The farther you are from your target, however, the worse the aiming accuracy will be when using an SMG. A Common-ranked Suppressed Submachine Gun is shown here. It's one of several types of SMGs typically available on the island.

Instead of holding down the trigger and utilizing Automatic Firing mode, SMGs tend to be more accurate if you use Burst mode. In other words, press the trigger for a second or two, release, and then press the trigger again, instead of holding it down.

Don't forget, within each weapon or gun category there are multiple types of weapons. Each weapon type is rated based on its color-coded Rarity (Common, Uncommon, Rare, Epic, or Legendary). A weapon's Rarity helps to determine its overall power and capabilities based on criteria, such as its Damage Per Second (DPS), overall Damage capabilities, Fire Rate, Magazine (Mag) Size, and Reload Time.

If you're carrying a specific weapon that you really like, and it's rated as Rare, for example, but you're able to find the same weapon, and the new one is ranked as Epic or Legendary, always swap it out for the more powerful version of the weapon, unless you have room in your inventory for both weapons. Later, when you need to get rid of a weapon to make room for something else, drop or swap out the weakest weapon(s) you have.

At any given time, more than 100 different weapon styles and variations are available on the island. With each new game update or gaming season, new weapons are introduced, others are removed altogether, and some have their capabilities tweaked—making them either more powerful or less powerful.

Where to Find Weapons on the Island

The arsenal a soldier carries must be collected and managed by the gamer controlling that soldier. With limited space in a soldier's inventory, it's important to maintain an arsenal that's useful for the types of fighting situations and terrain types you're currently facing during a match. It's very common for a gamer to slowly but dramatically alter their soldier's weapons arsenal as each match progresses.

Weapons (and ammo) can be found lying on the ground, out in the open. These are often found within buildings or structures, but sometimes outside.

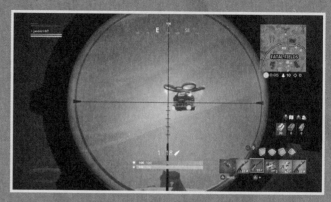

Opening chests is another way to build your soldier's arsenal. Chests have a golden glow and make a unique sound that can be heard from a distance. You'll often hear the sound emanating from a chest before you can see it, especially if the chest is located behind a wall, or above (or below) your soldier who is exploring a multi-level structure.

Added to Fortnite: Battle Royale *during Season 9, Loot Carriers work just like Supply Drops, but it's necessary to shoot them out of the sky in order to collect the random selection of weapons and/or loot items being carried within them. These Loot Carriers are drones that fly overhead during matches, so keep your eyes peeled!*

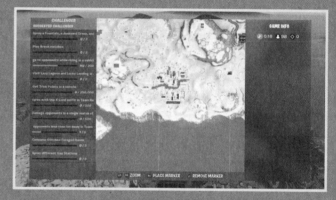

Supply Drops are rare and randomly drop from the sky. These tend to include powerful and rare weapons. However, to grab them, you must be the first person to arrive at and open the Supply Drop's wooden crate.

On the Island Map, points of interest that are labeled in yellow (in this case Happy Hamlet) indicate where you're most apt to find Loot Carriers randomly flying around. When on the island, you'll see these drones flying at all altitudes—some are high up and require a gun to shoot them down. Some Loot Carriers, however, hover closer to the ground and can be destroyed using your soldier's Harvesting Tool. Shown here is a zoomed-in view of the Island Map.

A Loot Llama looks like a colorful piñata. They get randomly scattered throughout the island but are much rarer than chests or Supply Drops. They tend to contain a larger and more powerful selection of weapons, ammo, and loot items.

In addition to its color-coded Rarity, when you collect a weapon and view it on your soldier's inventory screen, you can see how much damage it can inflict on other soldiers and buildings, plus determine its Magazine (Mag) Size, Damage Per Second (DPS), and Reload Time. The selected weapon shown here is a Legendary Automatic Sniper Rifle. It's one of the most powerful and versatile types of Sniper Rifles available in the game because it has a large Magazine Size (16 shots) and a relatively quick Reload Time (3.4 seconds). It can shoot four rounds per second and has a DPS rating of 140.0. This is the best Sniper Rifle for newbs because it allows you to shoot sixteen rounds quickly before reloading.

Vending Machines are also a great source for acquiring powerful weapons (with compatible ammo) one at a time during a match. These too are randomly scattered throughout the island. Each Vending Machine offers a different inventory selection. Approach the Vending Machine and watch for the available items to be displayed. When an item appears that you want, press the Select button on your keyboard or controller.

Especially during the mid- to final stages of a match, one of the best ways to quickly and dramatically improve your soldier's arsenal is to fight and defeat enemy soldiers. As soon as a soldier is defeated, not only are they removed from the match instantly, but everything the deceased soldier was carrying falls to the ground and can be grabbed by any of the surviving soldiers. Even if you don't defeat an enemy, you can still grab what a fallen enemy leaves behind after they've lost a firefight against someone else.

Magazine (Mag) Size determines how many rounds of ammo a weapon can hold before a reload is required. DPS tells you how much damage the weapon can inflict per second, and Reload Time tells you how quickly it takes to reload the weapon after ammo is used up (assuming you have a supply of appropriate ammo in your soldier's arsenal to reload with).

To keep *Fortnite: Battle Royale* interesting and challenging, Epic Games is constantly adjusting what weapons are capable of, as well as what selection of weapons is available during the match. When a weapon gets "vaulted," this means it's been removed from the game either temporarily or permanently. If a weapon gets "nerfed," this means its capabilities have been reduced or weakened.

To stay up-to-date on all of the weapons currently available within *Fortnite: Battle Royale*, and to see the ratings for each weapon, check out any of these independent websites:

- **Fortnite Weapon Stats & Info**—https://fortnitestats.com/weapons
- **Gamepedia Fortnite Wiki**—https://fortnite.gamepedia.com/Fortnite_Wiki
- **GameSkinny Fortnite Weapons List**—www.gameskinny.com/9mt22/complete-fortnite-battle-royale-weapons-stats-list
- **Metabomb**—www.metabomb.net/fortnite-battle-royale/gameplay-guides/fortnite-battle-royale-all-weapons-tier-list-with-stats-14
- **Tracker Network (Fortnite)**—https://db.fortnitetracker.com/weapons

Access the soldier's inventory screen anytime it's safe to do so during a match to learn more about the weapons, ammo, tools, resources, and other items your soldier is currently carrying and has available to them. Highlight one of the slots to view details about a specific weapon, item, or ammo type on the left side of the screen. A blue, Rare-rated Combat Shotgun is the active (selected) weapon shown here.

During a match, your soldier can hold up to six weapons or items in their main inventory. A soldier's inventory slots are shown in the lower-right corner of the game screen on most gaming systems. Once weapons or items are stored within your soldier's inventory slots, from the inventory Screen you're able to rearrange their order and/or drop unwanted or no longer needed weapons and items.

When playing a Duos, Squads, or team-oriented match, one key strategy is sharing weapons, items, and ammo with your allies. This is done by dropping what you want to share at a partner, squad mate, or teammate's feet and allowing them to pick it up.

Choosing what to carry, based on the situation your soldier is, or will soon be, facing, is one of your ongoing responsibilities during a match. If you know you'll be exploring an area of the island that contains many structures, and within those structures you're likely to encounter enemies, this means you'll need to be prepared for close-range combat. However, there will be plenty of times during a match when the use of mid-range, long-range, or explosive weapons is much more appropriate.

What You Should Know About Ammunition

Keep in mind, each weapon type uses one of five types of ammunition offered within the game—Light Bullets, Medium Bullets, Heavy Bullets, Shells, or Rockets.

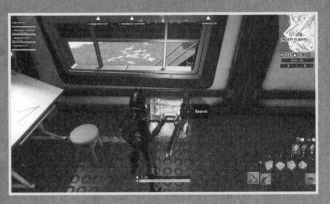

Chests, Loot Llamas, Loot Carriers, and Supply Drops are also sources of ammo. Plus, whenever you defeat an enemy soldier, you have the opportunity to grab some or all of the ammo that the defeated soldier leaves behind.

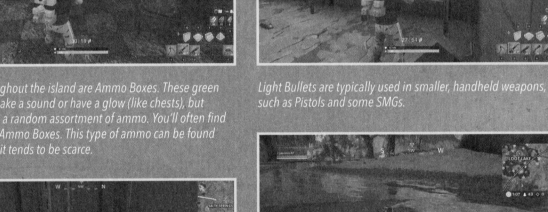

Scattered throughout the island are Ammo Boxes. These green boxes do not make a sound or have a glow (like chests), but they do contain a random assortment of ammo. You'll often find Rockets within Ammo Boxes. This type of ammo can be found elsewhere, but it tends to be scarce.

Light Bullets are typically used in smaller, handheld weapons, such as Pistols and some SMGs.

Look for Ammo Boxes on the ground and on shelves (within buildings). They're sometimes found on their own but can occasionally be found close to chests. If it's safe, always take the time to open and grab ammo from Ammo Boxes, as it's a quick and easy way to replenish your stash. Running out of bullets during a battle is one of the worst mistakes you can make when playing Fortnite: Battle Royale.

Medium Bullets cause more damage than Light Bullets. These are typically used within Assault Rifles and work particularly well when used at mid-range.

Heavy Bullets are used mainly in Sniper Rifles. These are the highest caliber ammo available on the island, and useful for reaching long-range targets. Weapons that use Heavy Bullets tend to have a low fire rate and long reload time, but they cause the most damage per shot when a direct hit is made.

Shells are used in various types of Shotguns. These weapons work well against close- to mid-range targets for a few reasons. For example, when as shell is shot from a Shotgun, the ammo splits apart into many tiny pieces. When those pieces hit one target, each piece of the shrapnel causes damage. If two targets are at close range, pieces from a single shell can hit and injure (or even defeat) multiple targets at once.

The drawback to a Shotgun that shoots Shells is that if you're too far away from your target when shooting this weapon, the Shell fragments have time to spread out a lot. Less of the ammo will hit your intended target, which means each hit causes much less damage. Plus, the farther away you are from your target when using a Shotgun, the less accurate your aim will be.

Rockets are a projectile and explosive type of ammo that get shot from a Rocket Launcher, Quad Launcher, Grenade Launcher, Boom Bow, or Guided Missile Launcher, for example. This type of ammo can be shot from a distance. It then explodes upon impact. Not only are Rockets useful for inflicting major damage on enemies, they can also be used to easily and quickly destroy structures or objects. Rockets are most commonly found within Ammo Boxes, as well as chests, Loot Llamas, and Supply Drops.

How to Accurately Aim and Fire Different Types of Weapons

Whenever you point an active weapon at any target, you'll see its targeting crosshairs. The smaller the crosshairs appear, the more accurate your shot will be. Typically, your bullets will land within the area depicted by the targeting crosshairs.

Standing still and crouching will reduce the size of the crosshairs, while walking, running, or jumping will increase the size of the crosshairs and greatly reduce your aiming accuracy.

Depending on the weapon, there are several ways to aim and then fire it. When any gun is active, point it toward your enemy and pull the trigger to fire it. This strategy works well when you're in close range, when time is more important than aiming accuracy because you're close to the enemy and it'll be difficult to miss your intended target. This is referred to as "shooting from the hip."

Simply by standing still, the targeting crosshairs for the weapon shrinks a lot, meaning that your soldier will be able to aim more accurately. To achieve the most precise aim, pressing the Aim button before pulling the trigger works best, but this takes slightly longer. If there were an enemy standing in front of him at close range, the fraction of a second it takes to press the Aim button could give the enemy the time needed to shoot their own weapon first.

By pressing the Aim button before pulling the trigger of a gun, you'll achieve more accurate aim for the weapon you're using, particularly if your soldier is crouching or standing still. Notice how small the targeting crosshair is that's displayed on the wall. You can barely make out the white "+". When you press the Aim button, the viewing perspective changes. You'll see your target from the end of a gun's barrel, and the target will appear closer.

Anytime you're using a weapon with a built-in scope, pressing the Aim button activates the scope and changes your view. The farther you are from your target, the more you may need to compensate for bullet drop, so aim slightly higher than your intended target. Learning to accurately account for bullet drop takes practice, and the technique varies for each type of long-range weapon.

Shown here, the soldier is running toward the building and is ready to fire his weapon. Notice the white aiming crosshairs (seen on the wall of the building) is very large. If he were to fire, the bullet would hit somewhere within this large crosshair area.

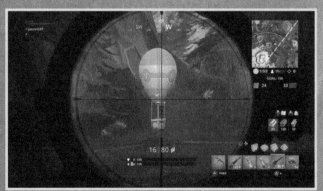

In this case, instead of running up to the Supply Drop and opening the crate to grab what's inside, the soldier chose to keep their distance and use a Sniper Rifle with a scope to aim at the Supply Drop, knowing that an enemy soldier would soon approach it. As soon as the enemy walks into the gun's targeting sight, they'll be shot. The Sniper Rifle's Scope view is shown here. As you can see, it allows you to really zoom in on a target and achieve highly accurate aim from a distance.

Consider using this strategy to easily pick off enemies who will likely stand still once they reach the Supply Drop (while they open the crate and collect what's inside). A stationary target is always much easier to aim at and hit. Keep in mind, achieving a headshot always causes the most damage, regardless of which weapon you use.

Be aware that when using many weapons, the longer you hold down the trigger to maintain continuous firing, the worse your soldier's aiming accuracy will be. You're better off tapping the trigger for a second or two and shooting short bursts of weapon fire, as opposed to holding down the trigger until the weapon needs to be reloaded.

Responsibility #2—Gather Resources

Building continues to be an important skill that's typically required to achieve #1 Victory Royale during a match. When it comes to building, your speed is as important as what you build. In order to build anything, however, your soldier must first gather resources (wood, stone, and metal).

Look for resource icons and grab them. Shown here is a Stone resource icon. As you can see, there's a small yellow and black banner that's within the banner describing the item. This particular resource icon is worth 30 Stone. Finding and grabbing these resource icons allows you to collect bundles of wood, stone, or metal that immediately get added to your soldier's inventory.

To harvest stone, use the Harvesting Tool to smash anything made of stone or brick that you find on the island, such as rock piles, brick walls (shown here), or any structures made from stone.

Using woods, stone, and metal resources that your soldier harvests using their Harvesting Tool, or collects during a match, they're able to build protective barriers, structures, ramps, bridges, and even elaborate fortresses. Shown here, wood is being harvested from trees using the soldier's Harvesting tool. To harvest wood, smash anything made of wood that you encounter on the island, including trees, some walls, wooden structures, or furniture.

Metal is the strongest material to build with. To harvest metal, smash anything made of metal that you come across while exploring the island, such as disabled vehicles, metal structures, or metal equipment (including appliances within a home). Anytime you smash a broken down vehicle using your soldier's Harvesting Tool, the vehicle's alarm will go off which generates a lot of noise. This will often attract the attention of nearby enemies.

Using the Harvesting Tool to smash metal appliances within a kitchen (found in any home) is an excellent source of metal.

Gamers develop their own unique strategies when it comes to building. Some people rely more heavily on building than others to achieve success during a match. At the very least, however, you must be able to build and edit basic structures quickly, especially during firefights when your soldier needs protection against incoming attacks or a safe place from which to launch attacks against enemies or reload their weapon(s).

Responsibility #3—Building

Once you understand what's possible using the building tools available, learning how to build (and edit the structures you build) extremely quickly will definitely give you an edge when playing *Fortnite*, especially during the End Game portion of a match.

In order to build, a soldier needs to switch from **Combat** mode to **Building** mode. While in **Building** mode, they're unable to use any weapons. Based on what resources your soldier has on hand, choose the best one to build with, and then mix and match the four different shaped building tiles available to construct whatever you need, where you need it.

Having a height advantage over your adversaries will prove beneficial in almost any combat situation during a match. Quickly being able to build ramps, bridges, structures, or fortresses to give your soldier a height advantage is often important.

Don't forget, it's possible to build almost anywhere on the island, including directly on top of existing structures, inside existing structures, or at the top of a hill or mountain. Especially if you have a long-range weapon, such as a Rocket Launcher or Sniper Rifle, consider building a fortress or small structure to give your soldier a height advantage, and then launch successful long-range attacks while being able to hide behind a protective barrier.

There are four different building tile shapes you can work with, including: horizontal floor/ceiling tiles, vertical wall tiles, ramp/stair-shaped tiles, and pyramid-shaped tiles. Each tile type can be constructed using wood, stone, or metal. Mix and match the building tiles to create custom-designed structures and fortresses.

information multiple times in the past, so when you play *Fortnite: Battle Royale*, the HP strength of each tile may vary.

TILE SHAPE	WOOD	STONE	METAL
Horizontal Floor/Ceiling Tile	140 HP	280 HP	460 HP
Vertical Wall Tile	150 HP	300 HP	500 HP
Ramp/Stairs Tile	140 HP	280 HP	460 HP
Pyramid-Shaped Tile	140 HP	280 HP	460 HP

Wood is the fastest material to build with but is the weakest in terms of offering any type of protection against attacks. Stone is stronger than wood but takes more time to build with. The strongest building material at your disposal is metal. It takes the longest to build with.

The following chart shows the maximum HP for each type of building tile you can work with. Keep in mind, Epic Games has tweaked this

Ramps and bridges should be constructed using wood, since they typically won't need to offer protection, and it's important to build this type of structure quickly, especially when you're engaged in combat and need to establish a height advantage over your enemy, or your soldier needs to travel to the top or bottom of a hill, mountain, or structure quickly.

Here, from left to right, vertical wall tiles have been constructed from wood, stone, and metal, respectively.

Each building tile has its own HP meter. When that tile's HP meter hits zero, as a result of being damaged from a Harvesting Tool, weapon, or explosive attack, that tile will be destroyed. A soldier has the ability to repair a damaged tile (which requires additional resources). As damage is inflicted on a building tile, it will become translucent and its HP meter will decrease. Shown here is a brick (stone) wall with its full 300 HP intact.

When a ramp/stair-shaped building tile is selected, a ramp is automatically created when wood is used. Stairs are created when either stone or metal is used.

Several shots have been fired on the brick (stone) wall. Its HP meter is currently at 100 HP out of 300 HP. When a tile is translucent (meaning it's been damaged), you can see through it, however, your enemies can see through it as well.

Pyramid-shaped tiles can be used as a roof of a building or structure or placed within a building or structure to provide a protective barrier or additional shielding from incoming attacks.

Using the Editing tools available while in Building mode, it's possible to build a window or door (shown here), for example, into a vertical or horizontal building tile. When you do this, the maximum HP for that tile will be reduced slightly.

Shown here, a window was built by editing this metal vertical wall tile.

If your soldier is being shot at and you need to build a quick structure for protection, first build a horizontal wall-shaped tile out of stone or metal. Immediately behind it, build a stairs tile, also out of stone or metal. Your soldier can now crouch down behind the stairs. An incoming attack will first need to go through two building tiles before reaching your soldier.

Shown here, a side wall was built to the simple metal structure, and the soldier is able to crouch behind it in order to avoid incoming fire and/or safely reload their weapon once its magazine is emptied.

Responsibility #4—Explore the Island

The mysterious island where every Fortnite: Battle Royale match takes place features approximately 20 labeled points of interest (locations), along with areas, structures, and buildings in between those points of interest. This is what the Island Map looked like midway through Season 10. At the start of season 11, Epic Games introduces some dramatic alternations to the island map, giving gamers many new and interesting places to explore.

Between the weekly game updates and the major updates made by Epic Games in between gaming seasons, the island and its terrain are constantly evolving. New points of interest are periodically added to the Island Map, while others are removed or dramatically altered.

At the start of each match, all 100 soldiers start in the pre-deployment area.

Once everyone has joined the match, the soldiers all board the flying Battle Bus. As the blue-colored bus follows a random route over the island, one of the first decisions you'll need to make is when and where your soldier should leap from the Battle Bus to begin their freefall toward land.

Based on the strategies you plan to adopt once your soldier lands, the landing spot you choose is important. If you opt to land in the heart of a popular point of interest, you're virtually guaranteed to encounter enemies almost immediately. This means that as soon as your soldier lands, they must find and grab at least one weapon (and ammo) to defend themselves and potentially launch attacks.

By landing in a less popular, more remote part of the island (in between labeled points of interest, for example), your soldier will typically have more time to explore the area and build up their arsenal before encountering and having to engage enemies.

In general, the newest points of interest on the map tend to be the most popular landing spots. You'll also find that locations near the center of the Island Map tend to be popular, so upon landing, your chance of encountering enemies right away is pretty high.

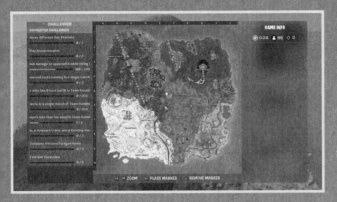 

While in the pre-deployment area before a match, or just after boarding the Battle Bus, if you check the Island Map, you'll see a line (comprised of tiny arrow icons) that show the random route and direction that Battle Bus will follow over the island. You can bet that locations near the very start and near the very end of the route will also be popular landing spots.

As the Battle Bus travels over the island, use the controller to rotate the view so you're able to see the back of the bus, as well as the soldiers leaping from the bus. This is one way you can gauge where your enemies will be landing.

During freefall from the bus, your soldier is able to glide and navigate a bit, so that while falling, you can also travel horizontally across up to about half the island.

Using the navigational controls, point your soldier in a straight downward direction to increase their freefall speed. This is useful if you need to reach the ground quickly to beat your enemies to a specific location.

At any time during freefall, you're able to manually deploy your soldier's Glider. This slows down their rate of descent and improves your navigational control. As land quickly approaches, however, your soldier's Glider will automatically deploy to ensure a safe landing.

Depending on where you land and whether or not enemies are nearby, your first objective should be to find and grab weapons, and then to begin exploring the island. Unless your soldier has taken cover behind a solid object (or structure you've built) that offers protection, keep your soldier moving to avoid becoming an easy target. Avoid walking or running in a straight line. Instead, randomly zigzag and jump to be as unpredictable as possible while in motion. This also applies when driving any type of vehicle.

Anytime your soldier is out in the open, enemy attacks can come from any direction—including above you, so be prepared to take cover, take evasive maneuvers, or quickly build a structure for protection.

The type of weapon you should have in-hand while exploring the island at any given time should be based on the type of terrain you're currently in and the challenges you're facing (or are about to face). While inside of many types of buildings, structures, caves, or tunnels, for example, close-range combat will be necessary.

In larger buildings, be prepared for close-to-mid-range combat. Anytime your soldier is outside, in the open, long-range combat is often safer and beneficial, but if enemies get too close, you'll need to contend with those threats as well.

As you explore the island, just about any building or object can be destroyed—including enemy fortresses or buildings enemies are hiding in. Explosive weapons work best for destroying buildings and objects. However, if you keep firing almost any type of gun at a building or structure, it'll cause damage and its eventual destruction—once the building, object, or structure's HP has been depleted.

There Are Many Transportation Options on the Island

The slowest way to get around the island is on foot. Your soldier can walk, run, crouch (tiptoe), or jump.

As you explore the island, you'll also encounter an ever-changing selection of vehicles your soldier can commandeer and drive.

At the start of Season 10 (also referred to as Season X), two popular vehicles—Quadcrashers and Ballers—were removed from the main game play modes of *Fortnite: Battle Royale*, but these vehicles could be re-introduced into the game at any time.

Some vehicles are great for outrunning or escaping from the storm, while others are better suited for moving directly toward an enemy to launch attacks. Vehicles also allow your

soldier to quickly evade incoming attacks or quickly move around the island.

A hoverboard (also referred to as a Driftboard) allows a soldier to travel fast across almost any type of terrain. The benefit to this vehicle is that when a soldier goes airborne, they're guaranteed to have a safe landing. One drawback, however, is that while on a hoverboard, a soldier is not shielded in any way against incoming attacks. While riding on this type of vehicle, a soldier can use any weapon or almost any item.

A hoverboard can help you climb up steep mountains or glide over water without slowing down. Use the vehicle's Boost feature to your advantage to quickly (but temporarily) pick up speed when needed. The better you become at driving the vehicle your soldier is using, the more useful the vehicle will become during a match.

Every season, you'll discover several other transportation options throughout the island. For example, a network of Ziplines may cover major areas of the island to provide an easy way to travel from one location to the next.

The island also often contains natural phenomenon, such as Geysers or Rifts (shown here), that a soldier can jump into in order to go airborne and then quickly travel from one area of the island to another. Again, these transportation options vary from season to season, so it's important to discover what options are available, and then choose the best times to use them.

How to Take Advantage of Map Coordinates and Markers

To make finding specific areas on the map easier, use the map coordinates system. Notice that along the top of the Island Map screen are the letters "A" through "J," and along the left edge of the map are the numbers "1" through "10." Anytime you need to identify a location on the map, use its coordinates.

During Season 10, Dusty Depot (a popular location that was removed previously) was returned to the island between map coordinates F5 and G5. Meanwhile, Neo Tilted was completely redesigned thanks to a time rift that was introduced. It was renamed Tilted Town and could be found at map coordinates D5 during Season 10.

Also during this season, Snobby Shores was located at map coordinates A5, and Retail Row was located at map coordinates H5.5. Lazy Lagoon could be found near map coordinates F3, and Pleasant Park was at map coordinates C3.5.

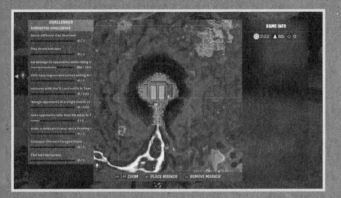

While you're looking at the Island Map, it's possible to zoom in on any location to see more detail. When looking at the main game screen, near the top-center of the screen is a compass display that can also be used to help you navigate around the island.

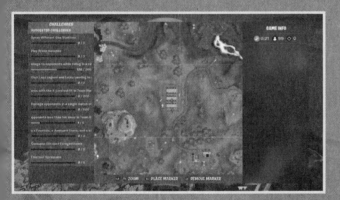

Markers can be placed on the Island Map. At the start of a match, while you're still in the pre-deployment area, or while riding on the Battle Bus, placing a Marker on the map shows your partner or squad mates where you intend to land, and allows you to quickly set a rendezvous location without having to talk. Using the zoom feature on the Island Map, Dusty Depot is shown here. There's a blue Marker located within this point of interest. You, as well as your partner or squad mates, can all add different-colored Markers to the Island Map screen, as needed.

Once one or more Markers have been placed on the map screen, they're displayed as colored flares on the main game screen, and they can be seen from great distances. Even if you're playing a Solo match, and you know you're trying to reach a specific location, placing a Marker on the Island Map makes that location easier to see from a distance when you're navigating your way to it.

Keep in mind, whenever you place a Marker on the Island Map, only you, your partner, and/or your Squad Mates can see it. Gamers controlling enemy soldiers cannot see your Marker(s). Upon reaching a location that's been marked on the map, the colored flare on the main game screen (and its related Marker on the Island Map) will automatically disappear. As you're approaching a Marker, however, the distance between your soldier's current location and that Marker is displayed on the screen.

Responsibility #5—Avoid the Deadly Storm

As if dealing with up to 99 enemies on the island wasn't enough, within minutes after your soldier's arrival, a deadly storm forms and begins to expand, until it eventually engulfs almost the entire island during the final minutes of a match (when only a few soldiers remain alive).

Displayed below the mini-map on the main game screen is a timer that tells you when the storm will form, or when it will next expand and move. In this case, the storm will expand and move again in 19 seconds.

Within the mini-map, follow the white line to discover the shortest route between your current location on the island and the next safe zone (which is the area not yet made uninhabitable by the storm).

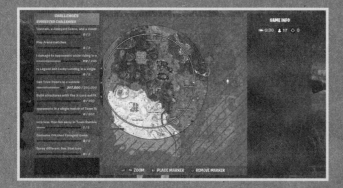

Shown here is the Island Map view of the soldier's current location (near map coordinates G5). The outer circle shows the current safe zone, the inner circle shows where the next safe zone will be, and the area in pink shows the storm-ravaged areas of the island. Your soldier's current location is displayed as a small white arrow icon when playing Solo mode. The color of the icon will vary if you're playing a Duos or Squads match, for example.

Both within the mini-map, as well as on the Island Map screen, the areas of the island shown in pink have already been made uninhabitable by the storm. Anytime you see two circles displayed on the Island Map, the outer circle in the current safe area, and the inner (smaller) circle shows you where the safe region will be once the deadly storm expands and moves again.

While exploring the island, the edge of the storm is depicted as a blue wall. As long as you stay on the safe side of the blue wall (within the safe zone circle depicted on the map), your biggest concern will be the enemy soldiers remaining on the island who are trying to eliminate your soldier from the match. Shown here, the soldier is standing on the safe side of the storm's blue wall.

For each second your soldier finds themselves on the wrong side of the blue wall and caught within the deadly storm, some of their Health meter will be depleted. Once your soldier's Health meter reaches zero, they will immediately be eliminated from the match.

If your soldier enters the storm-ravaged area during the early stages of the match, the speed that their Health meter will be depleted starts off slow. Later in the match, your soldier will receive greater damage to their Health meter faster. On most gaming systems a soldier's Health and Shield meters are displayed near the bottom-center of the screen. When playing on an iPad, for example, these meters can be found near the top-left corner of the screen, next to the mini-map.

There will be times when your soldier has to travel a far distance from the currently safe area to what will be the new safe region once the storm expands and moves again. You'll discover it's very difficult (and sometimes impossible) to outrun the storm for an extended amount of time, unless your soldier is riding in a vehicle or utilizing some other mode of transportation on the island. Driving or riding in a vehicle is typically the fastest and easiest way to travel around the island and successfully outrun the movement of the storm.

Remember, Shields do not protect your soldier from damage caused by the storm, or injury incurred as the result of a fall. Shields do, however, offer protection from incoming weapon attacks and explosions.

Responsibility #6—Engage in Combat and Defeat Your Enemies

Finding and collecting a powerful arsenal of weapons and ammo is important, but even more essential is knowing how to use each type of weapon so that you can defend your soldier and launch highly effective attacks against your enemies.

Achieving #1 Victory Royale requires you to defeat enemies during matches. However, based on the strategies you choose to adopt, you may focus more on survival and exploration during a match, as opposed to eliminating as many enemy soldiers as possible.

Some gamers love to jump right into the combat action and engage in as many firefights and battles as they can. While defeating enemies will help you boost your Season Level when playing *Fortnite: Battle Royale*, there are other ways to achieve this that focus less on combat.

Assuming you're trying to complete all 100 Tiers of a particular Battle Pass, the Missions and Challenges you'll be faced with often require you to use a particular type of weapon or item to successfully eliminate one or more enemies in a particular combat situation. Thus, you'll definitely want to review the available Challenges displayed prior to a match on the left side of the Lobby screen or the Island Map screen, so you can work toward achieving them during the matches you participate in.

The currently available Challenges are also displayed when you select the Challenges tab at the top of the Lobby screen, select the Event, Missions, or Style tab (in the top-center of the Challenges screen), and then select one of the displayed Missions or banners to see the individual descriptions of the Challenges.

The better acquainted you become with each type of weapon available in your soldier's arsenal, and the more practice you have under your belt using each type of weapon, the bigger advantage you'll gain during a match. Don't forget, choosing the right weapon for the task at hand is always important.

During every match, each soldier is being controlled by a different gamer. Some players will be more experienced and have better skills than you, while others will be easier to defeat. While trying to be as unpredictable as possible when controlling your soldier, try to figure out patterns or strategies your adversaries are using, so you can accurately predict what they'll do next or how they'll respond in specific situations.

Also, keep in mind that sound plays an important role when playing *Fortnite: Battle Royale*! Make sure you're able to hear the sound effects clearly. You'll often hear enemies or danger approaching before you can see it, so listen carefully for weapons fire, footsteps, the sound of building, noise generated by vehicles, and the sound of doors opening or closing, for example.

Pay Attention to Your Soldier's Health and Shield Meters

Displayed near the bottom-center of the screen on most gaming systems are your soldier's Health and Shield meters.

At the start of a match, your soldier's Health meter will be at 100 percent. Each time they receive damage as a result of an attack, fall, getting caught in an explosion, or wind up within the storm, for example, some (or in some cases all) of their Health gets depleted.

As soon as a soldier's Health meter hits zero, they're immediately eliminated from the match. Remember, if you're playing a Duos or Squads match, for example, an ally has 90 seconds to grab your soldier's Reboot Card and return it to a Respawn Van (shown here), which allows the eliminated soldier to be returned to a match. Successfully reaching a Respawn Van can be a challenge if it's being guarded by enemies.

There are many ways to replenish your soldier's Health meter during a match. For example, you can activate a Campfire that you discover on the island, or you can use a Cozy Campfire item. A Cozy Campfire item is shown here.

As you explore the island, be on the lookout for these Campfires, which you can light manually in order to replenish some of your soldier's Health meter. Light the Campfire and then stand close to the flame. Keep in mind, multiple soldiers (including your partner, squad mates, or teammates) can all benefit simultaneously by standing close to the flame of a lit Campfire or Cozy Campfire.

During each gaming season, there are an assortment of Health replenishment items that can be found, collected, stored within your soldier's inventory, and then used when needed. Others can be found and consumed immediately (but can't be collected and stored).

The following chart describes many of the popular Health replenishment items available within *Fortnite: Battle Royale*. Keep in mind, the selection of items offered changes with each new gaming season, so not all of items listed here will be available when you play.

Fortnite: Battle Royale's Health Replenishment Items

HEALTH ITEM	HOW LONG IT TAKES TO USE OR CONSUME	POWERUP BENEFIT	STORAGE LOCATION	MAXIMUM NUMBER YOU CAN CARRY
Apples	Instant	Restore 5 HP to a soldier's Health meter instantly.	Must be consumed when and where they're found.	Not Applicable
Bananas	Instant	Restores 5 HP to a soldier's Health meter when consumed.	Must be consumed when and where they're found.	Not Applicable
Bandages	4 Seconds	Boost a soldier's Health meter by 15 HP (up to 75 HP)	Requires one backpack inventory slot.	15
Chug Jug	15 Seconds	Replenishes a soldier's Health *and* Shield meters back to 100.	Requires one backpack inventory slot.	1
Chug Splash	Instant	Boosts Health *or* Shield HP by 25. This item gets smashed. To benefit, a soldier must be within the radius of the splash zone.	Requires one backpack inventory slot.	6
Coconuts	Instant	Restores 5 HP to a soldier's Health meter when consumed. If their Health meter is at 100, 5 HP is added to their Shield meter.	Must be consumed when and where they're found.	Not Applicable
Cozy Campfire	25 Seconds	Boosts a soldier's Health meter by 2 HP per second for up to 25 seconds.	Gets stored in a soldier's inventory with Ammo and Resources.	Not Applicable
Med Kit	10 Seconds	Boosts a soldier's Health meter back to 100 HP	Requires one backpack inventory slot.	3

HEALTH ITEM	HOW LONG IT TAKES TO USE OR CONSUME	POWERUP BENEFIT	STORAGE LOCATION	MAXIMUM NUMBER YOU CAN CARRY
Pepper	Instant	Restores 5 HP to a soldier's Health meter and increases their movement speed by 20 percent for 10 seconds.	Must be consumed when and where they're found.	Not Applicable
Slurp Juice	25 Seconds	Boosts a soldier's Health *and* Shield meter by 1 HP per second for 25 seconds.	Requires one backpack inventory slot.	2

Bandages are just one of the available items that can be used to replenish some of your soldier's Health during a match.

Keep a Med Kit in your soldier's arsenal so you can quickly return their Health meter to 100 HP if they incur damage during a battle.

A Legendary Chug Jug offers the ultimate Health and Shield boost. It returns both meters to 100 HP in just 15 seconds. Make sure your soldier hides or is safely behind a barricade before activating a Health or Shield replenishment item that takes several seconds to consume or use. While one of these items is being used, a soldier must stand still and cannot use a weapon to defend themselves or launch an attack.

This soldier is about to pick up a Slurp Juice. It will get stored within one of their inventory slots until it's needed.

Initially when a match kicks off, a soldier's Shields meter is at zero. To activate your soldier's Shields, use any Shield replenishment item, such as a Small Shield Potion, Shield Potion (shown here), Chug Jug, or Mushrooms. Once activated, Shields will protect your soldier against incoming gun fire and explosions, but not against falls or damage caused by the storm. If your soldier is hit by incoming gunfire or an explosion, for example, first their Shield meter gets depleted, followed by their Health meter. Items like a Shield Potion can be found, collected, stored in your soldier's inventory, and then used as needed. Other items, like Mushrooms, need to be consumed where they're found.

In addition to using Health-related items to keep your soldier's Health meter at 100 percent,

there are also Shield-related items used for activating and replenishing your soldier's Shield meter.

Achieving success when playing *Fortnite: Battle Royale* relies on participating in combat. Thus, it's essential to activate and maintain your soldier's Shields, since they offer added protection against incoming attacks. It's always a good idea to boost Shields to 100 percent before a battle, and to replenish your soldier's Shields immediately after a battle.

It takes a few seconds to use or consume most Shield-related items, during which time your soldier must stand still. They can't simultaneously use a weapon or build, so they're somewhat vulnerable to attack. As a result, it's best to consume or use a Shield-related item when you know your soldier is safe from enemy attacks.

Fortnite: Battle Royale's Shield-Related Items

SHIELD ITEM	HOW LONG IT TAKES TO USE OR CONSUME	POWERUP BENEFIT	STORAGE LOCATION	MAXIMUM NUMBER YOU CAN CARRY
Chug Jug	15 seconds	Replenishes your soldier's Health *and* Shield meters to 100.	Requires one backpack inventory slot.	1
Coconuts	Almost Instantly	Increase your soldier's Health meter by 5 points per Coconut that's consumed. However, if your soldier's Health meter is at 100, their Shield meter will receive some replenishment.	Coconuts must be consumed when and where they're found. They cannot be carried and used later.	None
Mushrooms	Almost instantly	Increase your soldier's Shield meter by 5 points (up to 100).	Mushrooms must be consumed when and where they're found. They cannot be carried and used later.	None

SHIELD ITEM	HOW LONG IT TAKES TO USE OR CONSUME	POWERUP BENEFIT	STORAGE LOCATION	MAXIMUM NUMBER YOU CAN CARRY
Shield Bubble	Instant	When active, this item creates a Shield around your soldier that offers 400 HP worth of protection against incoming attacks for up to 30 seconds. If the 400 HP get depleted sooner, however, the Shield Bubble gets destroyed and deactivates. Weapon fire and explosives can't penetrate a Shield Bubble, but enemy soldiers can walk into it and attack from within the bubble.	This item must be found, collected, and stored in one of your soldier's inventory slots until it's needed and activated.	Undisclosed
Shield Potion	5 seconds	Replenishes your soldier's Shield meter by 50 points (up to 100 maximum).	Requires one backpack inventory slot.	2
Slurp Juice	Approximately 2 seconds to consume and 37.5 seconds to achieve its full benefit.	For 37.5 seconds, a soldier's Health *and* Shield meters increase by one point (up to 75 points) every half-second after the drink is consumed.	Requires one backpack inventory slot.	1
Small Shield Potion	2 seconds	Replenishes your soldier's Shield meter by 25 points.	Requires one backpack inventory slot.	10

Responsibility #7—Complete Battle Pass–Related Missions and Challenges

If you opt to purchase a Battle Pass, each time you participate in a match during any gaming season, in addition to the other six main responsibilities you'll need to juggle, you'll also want to strive toward completing Missions and Challenges associated with the Battle Pass. By completing Missions and Challenges, you'll receive Battle Stars. These are used to unlock Battle Pass Tiers.

At the start of Season 10, Missions were introduced into *Fortnite: Battle Royale*, while daily and weekly challenges were eliminated or restructured.

As you'll discover, each season's Battle Pass includes 100 different Tiers you'll need to unlock in order to receive their Rewards. This will require you to complete Missions that include specific tasks.

The only time limit for completing the Battle Pass–related tasks is the duration of the gaming season. At the end of the gaming season, the Battle Pass ends, whether or not you have completed all of the Missions and Challenges.

Of course, if you discover the gaming season is coming to an end too soon, and you still have a bunch of Tier-based Challenges to complete, but there's not enough time to complete them, one option is to pay V-Bucks to unlock the Rewards associated with individual Tiers. The cost is 150 V-Bucks per Tier (approximately $1.50 US).

Alternatively, if you purchase a basic Battle Pass for 950 V-Bucks (approximately $9.50 US), you can then pay 15,000 V-Bucks (approximately $150.00 US) to unlock all of the Battle Pass Tiers and instantly receive all of the Rewards associated with that Battle Pass. It's much more fun

(and far less expensive), however, to purchase the Battle Pass and then complete the Battle Pass Missions and Challenges yourself.

A typical *Fortnite: Battle Royale* gaming season lasts between 10 and 12 weeks, so if you purchase a Battle Pass at the start of a season, you'll have plenty of time to complete all of the Missions and Challenges.

As you can see here by looking near the top-left corner of the Battle Pass Tier grid, there are still 41 days remaining in this gaming season, and the player has already reached and unlocked Battle Pass Tier Level 62. Moving forward, if the player completes Challenges to unlock just 10 Battle Stars per day, they'll be able to reach Tier 100 with no problem whatsoever.

Options for Customizing Your Soldier

Prior to starting each match, you have the option to customize the appearance of your soldier from the Locker. This is what the main Locker screen looks like.

After accessing the Locker from the Lobby, one at a time, choose a soldier's Outfit (shown here), Back Bling (backpack) design, Harvesting tool design, Glider design, and Contrail design.

Also from the Locker, be sure to select up to six different Emotes (including dance moves) that you want your soldier to be able to perform during the upcoming match. Only Emotes that have been previously unlocked or purchased are available from the Locker.

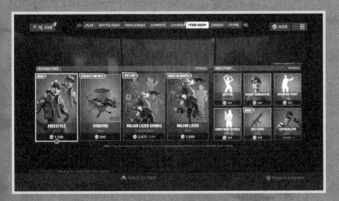

Most items that become available in your soldier's Locker must be purchased from the Item Shop (using V-Bucks which cost real money) or somehow unlocked by completing in-game Challenges or Missions.

Customizing your soldier offers no tactical advantage during a match, but most gamers love to alter the appearance of the soldier they're controlling, and be able to choose the selection of Emotes that can be used to taunt enemies and communicate with them while in the pre-deployment area or during a match.

Several independent websites offer detailed information about all of the Outfits and items thus far released in *Fortnite*. Several of these websites are listed in *Section 5—Fortnite: Battle Royale Resources*, but you can start by visiting the continuously updated Fortnite *Skins*

List website from Pro Game Guides at https://progameguides.com/fortnite-skins-list (shown here) or the Fortnite *Skins* website at https://fortniteskins.net/outfits.

Read Up on Battle Passes

Get the latest information on battle passes with books like the unofficial *Master Combat* series. Each guide in this series focuses on specific aspects of *Fortnite* and is chock full of game play strategies, survival tips, and information you'll need to improve your gaming skills.

To learn about the other books in this popular series, be sure to visit **www.ForniteGameBooks .com**.

As you're about to discover, *Battle Pass Success for Fortniters: An Unofficial Guide to Battle Royale*

focuses on purchasing and experiencing an optional Battle Pass that Epic Games offers in conjunction with each new gaming season of *Fortnite: Battle Royale*.

A Battle Pass is an optional purchase that costs real money. A new Battle Pass is introduced at the start of each gaming season. Each Battle Pass includes 100 Tiers.

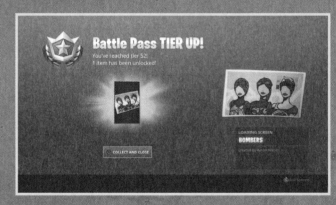

As soon as you complete the Missions and Challenges required to collect the right number of Battle Stars, you'll be able to unlock one Battle Pass Tier at a time and receive a Reward for your accomplishment. A variety of different types of Rewards are offered throughout each gaming season.

If you can't (or don't want to) complete a specific Mission or Challenge, you can either spend additional money to unlock one Battle Pass Tier at a time or seek out the assistance of your online friends to help you accomplish specific objectives.

Fortnite: Battle Royale Is Always Evolving

One reason why *Fortnite: Battle Royale* has become a true global phenomenon is that anyone can play the game on their Windows PC, Mac, Playstation 4, Xbox One, Nintendo Switch, Apple iPhone, Apple iPad, or on many Android-based mobile devices.

As new gaming systems are released in 2020 and beyond by Sony, Microsoft, Nintendo, and Google, for example, a version of *Fortnite: Battle Royale* will likely be released for each of these new systems, giving even more gamers full access to this mega-popular "battle royale" gaming experience.

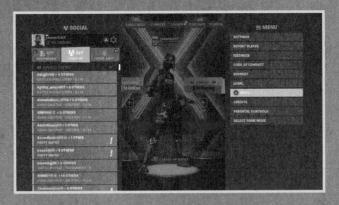

At any time, from the Fortnite: Battle Royale *Lobby, access the Game Menu (shown here) and select the News option (seen on the right side of the screen) to discover what's new in the game. To access this menu, click on the Game Menu icon that's displayed in the top-right corner of the Lobby screen.*

Regardless of which gaming system you use to experience Fortnite: Battle Royale, *each week, Epic Games releases a game update, which is called a patch. An update might include a small change to the Island Map, the introduction of one or more new weapons, changes to existing weapons, or the introduction (or removal) of specific items. To discover what's new each week, be sure to read the News screen that's displayed when you launch* Fortnite: Battle Royale.

Using your favorite web browser, be sure to visit the official Fortnite: Battle Royale *website (www.fortnite.com/news) and read the News section. There are also many independent websites, some of which are listed within Section 5—Fortnite: Battle Royale Resources, that will keep you up to date on the latest news and information related to what's happening within the game.*

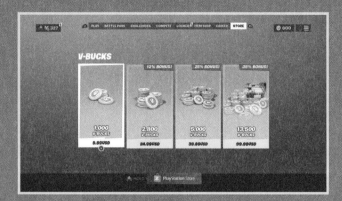

Items that are made available from the Item Shop are purchased using V-Bucks, which is Fortnite's in-game currency used to make purchases. Acquiring V-Bucks is done from the Store (shown here).

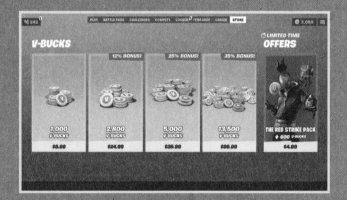

At least once or twice per gaming season, Epic Games offers a special Bundle Pack from the Store (not the Item Shop) that includes an exclusive Outfit, plus a bundle of V-Bucks. Sometimes, a matching Back Bling design, Harvesting Tool design, and/or Glider design is also included. Plan on spending $4.99 (US) or $9.99 (US) for one of these special bundles. Outfits, for example, that are included within these bundles are offered for a limited time, and never re-released.

Once you've played *Fortnite: Battle Royale* for multiple seasons, you'll notice that while all Battle Passes include 100 Tiers, what you need to accomplish in order to unlock each Tier varies greatly. In addition, the assortment of Rewards (prizes) offered for unlocking Battle Pass Tiers and completing Missions and Challenges also changes. Keep in mind, completing Battle Pass Missions and Challenges continues to be one of the best ways to unlock and collect exclusive

soldier Outfits and Emotes, for example, that are not available from the Item Shop or elsewhere.

Each season, Epic Games includes multiple exclusive soldier Outfits as prizes for completing the various Missions and Challenges. In conjunction with Season 10, for example, the Outfits that could be unlocked from the season's Battle Pass included: X-Lord, Catalyst, Tilted Teknique, Yond3R (shown here), Sparkle Supreme, Eternal Voyager, and Ultima Knight.

Outfits that are part of a season's Battle Pass are only available during that season, and they're never sold within the Item Shop. In addition to the exclusive Outfits that are part of a Battle Pass, a selection of Outfit Styles are offered as separate Tier-related prizes and Style-related Challenge Rewards.

An Outfit Style allows you to alter the appearance of an Outfit that you've already unlocked and that's available within your soldier's Locker. Some Outfits have multiple Styles that can be unlocked separately as part of Battle Pass Tier-based challenges or separate Style Challenges that are featured within the game.

While purchasing and experiencing a Battle Pass each gaming season is optional, most gamers agree that the added Missions and Challenges (and the Rewards offered) make *Fortnite: Battle Royale* even more fun and challenging, whether you prefer the Solo, Duos, Squads, or limited-time game play modes that *Fortnite: Battle Royale* has to offer.

Assuming you've decided to purchase and activate the current Battle Pass that's being offered by Epic Games, the rest of this unofficial strategy guide will teach you everything you need to know about acquiring and experiencing Battle Passes when playing *Fortnite: Battle Royale*, regardless of the gaming season.

You'll learn all about what Battle Passes offer, the types of Rewards that can be unlocked, and how to take full advantage of those prizes during game play. Most importantly, you'll discover tips and strategies for completing the Missions and Challenges related to Battle Passes.

Regardless of which gaming season you're about to experience, prepare yourself for non-stop challenges, excitement, and fun as you strive to achieve #1 Victory Royale during each match you experience when playing *Fortnite: Battle Royale*!

Reap the Benefits of a Battle Pass

Especially when it comes to customizing the appearance of your soldier, working your way through the Tiers of a Battle Pass during any gaming season will help you expand the contents of your soldier's Locker. This includes allowing you to unlock new and exclusive Outfits, Back Bling designs, Harvesting Tool designs, Glider designs, Outfit Styles, weapon and vehicle Wraps, and Emotes (including dance moves and spray paint tags).

A basic Battle Pass costs 950 V-Bucks, which is equivalent to about $9.50 (US). At the end of each gaming season, the current Battle Pass will expire, but a new one will be released at the start of each new season.

All Battle Pass Rewards you unlock are yours to keep forever. Most get stored within your soldier's Locker. Items that remain locked at the end of a season, however, cannot be unlocked later, once a Battle Pass ends.

The Battle Pass Tier 100 Reward is always an ultra-exclusive, Legendary Outfit that's only available during one gaming season, so if you're looking to expand your soldier's Locker with a special Outfit, you'll definitely want to complete the Challenges necessary to unlock Battle Pass Tier 100 during each gaming season!

Now that you understand some of the basics for playing *Fortnite: Battle Royale*, you'll learn more about how to acquire a Battle Pass and participate in Missions and Challenges from the next several sections of this guide.

SECTION 2

FORTNITE: BATTLE ROYALE BATTLE PASSES, MISSIONS, AND CHALLENGES

Once you download and install *Fortnite: Battle Royale*, you can begin playing the game, for free and on an unlimited basis. However, if you want to customize your soldier in any way, you'll need to:

- Visit the Item Shop to purchase items using V-Bucks. (V-Bucks can be acquired in bundles from the Shop using real money).
- Complete various types of Free Pass, Event, Mission, and Style-based

Challenges to unlock Rewards. Especially if you've purchased the current season's Battle Pass, there are several categories of Missions and Challenges offered at any given time when playing Fortnite: Battle Royale.

- Request gifts from your online friends.
- Acquire and unlock items through some type of Epic Games promotion.
- Purchase a Battle Pass and complete the related Missions and Challenges.

Discover What Can Be Done from the Lobby

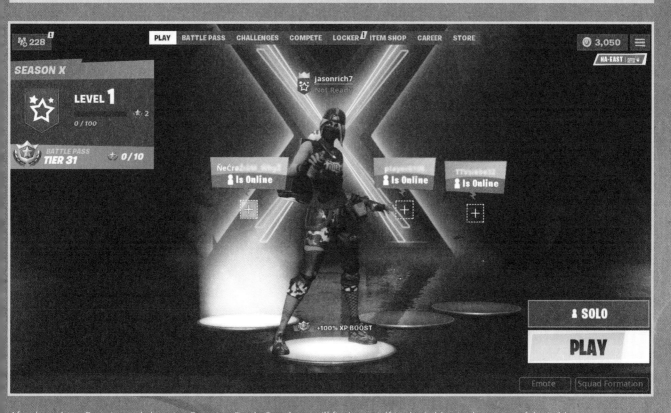

After launching Fortnite and choosing Fortnite: Battle Royale, *you'll find yourself in the Lobby. In the center of the Lobby screen is your soldier. In the lower-right corner (directly above the Play option), choose the Solo option to access the Game Play Mode menu. Keep in mind, the Solo option will display whichever match type you experienced last, so it might say Duos or Squads, for example. (Shown here on a PC.)*

From the Game Play Mode menu, choose between Solo, Duos, Squads, Playground, Creative, or one of the limited-time modes. If you've chosen Duos, Squads, or another game play mode that allows you to team up with one or more other gamers, select the Fill option to have the game randomly choose a partner or squad mates for you. (Shown here on a PS4.)

Displayed along the top of the Lobby screen are a series of menu icons, including: Play, Battle Pass, Challenges, Compete, Locker, Item Shop, Career, and Store. Clicking on each grants access to specific game play options. The Play option allows you to choose a game play mode (bottom-right corner), accept Invites from online friends (center), see a summary of currently available Missions and Challenges (left side), access the Social menu (top-left corner), and access the Game menu (top-right corner).

To send invites to your online friends, select the Don't Fill option then access the Social menu from the top-left corner of the Lobby. Select the Party Up tab at the top of the Social menu to send Invites and play with your online friends.

Click on the Battle Pass option to purchase a Battle Pass each season, purchase and unlock Battle Pass Tiers, gift Battle Passes to other people, and review all Battle Pass Rewards (prizes) for the current season. More information about purchasing and managing Battles Passes is found in Section 3—Everything You Need to Know About Acquiring a Battle Pass.

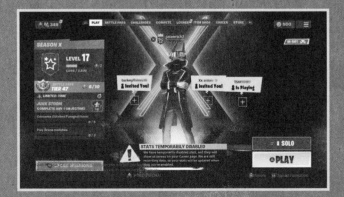

Invites you receive are displayed on the Lobby screen, as yellow banners that say "[Username] Invited You!". They're seen to the right and/or left of your soldier (who is positioned in the center).

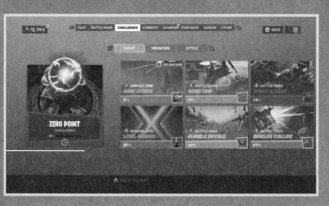

Starting in Season 10, Epic Games began offering an ongoing series of Event, Mission, and Style-related Missions and Challenges. (Daily, Weekly, and Tier-based Challenges were removed from the game.) To participate in some of these Missions and Challenges, acquiring a Battle Pass is required. Others are open to everyone. To discover all of the Challenges currently offered in Fortnite: Battle Royale, click on the Challenges tab at the top of Lobby screen.

It's from the Locker screen that you're able to customize the appearance of your soldier prior to a match. Click on the Locker tab to access it. As you can see, on the left side of the Locker screen are a series of slots. Each slot represents something that's customizable, based on the items you've unlocked, received, or purchased and that are stored within your soldier's Locker. In the top-left corner is the Outfit slot.

Leading up to the annual Fortnite World Cup competition, Epic Games hosts a series of tournaments throughout the year. To qualify for, and potentially compete in any of these tournaments, click on the Compete tab that's displayed at the top of the Lobby screen.

Click on the Outfit slot to choose your soldier's Outfit from all of the Outfits you've previously purchased, received, or unlocked.

To the right of the Outfit slot is the Back Bling slot. Click on this to select a backpack design for your soldier. To the right of the Back Bing slot, click on the Harvesting Tool slot to choose a Harvesting Tool design.

Moving to the right again, click on the Glider slot to choose your soldier's Glider design, based on Glider items you've purchased, received, or unlocked. Next click on the Contrail slot to choose your soldier's Contrail design.

The Contrail design is the animation you'll see emanating from your soldier's hands and/or feet as they freefall from the Battle Bus to the island at the start of a match. Shown here is a Contrail design called Lava.

The second row contains six slots. Each represents one type of Emote that your soldier can use in the pre-deployment area or anytime during a match.

There are several types of Emotes, including dance moves, spray paint tags, and toys. For each type of Emote, there's an ever growing selection that you can purchase, receive, or unlock, one at a time. For example, there are literally hundreds of different dance moves that have already been released. Shown here is a preview of a dance move Emote called Jaywalking.

Interactive Toys are another type of Emote that can be unlocked and used during a match for entertainment purposes. Toys cannot be used as weapons and have no impact on the combat aspect of matches. The Basketball Toy is shown here. It can be used at any of the basketball courts found on the island (or anywhere else for that matter). You could potentially throw a Basketball at an enemy during a match, but it will cause no harm whatsoever. A Toy can be used as a distraction tool, however, to create a diversion.

This is an example of a Spray Paint Tag that can be unlocked and then used to create graffiti on any flat surface while exploring the island, such as a wall or floor.

Emoticons are graphic icons that your soldier can toss into the air for everyone around them to see while in the pre-deployment area or during a match.

During any single match, your soldier can only access and use up to six different Emotes. Once the six Emotes are selected from the Locker, while in the pre-deployment area (shown here) or during a match, access this Emotes menu to choose, use, and showcase an Emote. If you're controlling the game using a keyboard/mouse combo (as opposed to a controller), press the keyboard key that's associated with an Emote to use it during a match.

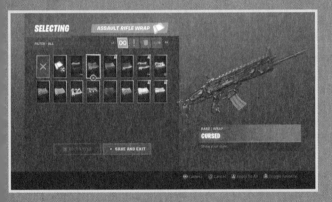

Every day, the Item Shop offers a different selection of Outfits, Harvesting Tool designs, Emotes, and other items that can be purchased using V-Bucks. Click on the Item Shop tab at the top of the Lobby screen to access the Item Shop.

Within the Locker, below the row of Emotes slots are multiple Wrap slots. Each allows you to choose a Wrap for a specific type of vehicle, item, or weapon. A Wrap is a graphic design that you can unlock or receive, that allows you to customize the appearance of weapons, vehicles, and certain other items in the game. Many different Wrap styles are available. Only the Wrap designs you've purchased, unlocked, or received will be accessible from the Locker.

The bottom row of three slots allow you to choose a custom banner, background music, and a loading screen graphic. Many gamers opt to turn off the music in the game to avoid distractions. At the same time, they turn up the volume of the game's sound effects. This is done from the Audio submenu within Settings.

Click on the Career tab to access a menu that allows you to customize and view your Profile, view the continuously updated Fortnite: Battle Royale Leaderboards, and watch recorded replays of your own matches.

It's from the Store that you're able to purchase bundles of V-Bucks. These are sold in bundles of 1,000 ($9.99 US), 2,800 ($24.99 US), 5,000 ($39.99 US), and 13,500 ($99.99 US). Periodically during each gaming season, a Limited Time Bundle is also offered.

As you can see here, The Red Strike Pack bundle ($4.99 US) available during Season 10 included 600 V-Bucks, the Epic Red Strike Outfit, and the Epic Bladed Bag Back Bling. When one of these Limited Time Bundles is available from the Store, click on the offer seen on the main Store screen, and then click on the Purchase button that's displayed.

Confirm your purchase decision by clicking on the Place Order button. If you purchased a Limited Time Bundle, the Outfit and related items will immediately be placed in your soldier's Locker. If you purchased a bundle of V-Bucks, these get added to your account. Your V-Buck Balance is displayed near the top-right corner of the Lobby screen.

The Game Menu

Displayed in the top-right corner of the Lobby screen is the Game Menu icon. It looks like three horizontal lines. Click on this icon to display the game's menu. It's seen on the right side of the screen. Menu options include: Settings, Report Player, Feedback, Code of Conduct, Support, Legal, News, Credits, Parental Controls, Select Game Mode, and Exit.

When you click on the Settings menu option, the game's Settings menu is displayed. Along the top of this menu are a bunch of command tabs. These will vary based on which gaming system you're using. On a PC, from left to right, each of these command tabs reveals a submenu, including: Video, Game, Brightness, Audio, Accessibility, Input, Controller, and Account. From the Video submenu (shown here), you're able to adjust various options related to graphics that get displayed on your computer's monitor during game play. This applies to PC and Mac gamers only.

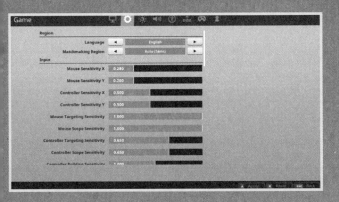

Click on the Game tab to access this Game submenu. From here, it's possible to tweak various settings to improve game controller (or mouse) sensitivity. You're also able to choose your Language and Matchmaking Region. Unless you specifically want to compete against gamers from another country (or part of your country), leave this setting on Auto to ensure the fastest response time from the Epic Games servers.

When playing Fortnite: Battle Royale using a controller, click on the Controller tab to choose one of the controller layouts (Old School, Quick Builder, Combat Pro, or Builder Pro), or select the Custom option to create your own controller layout for the controller you'll be using. (Shown here on a PS4. If you're using an Xbox One or Nintendo Switch, the controller options for your console-based system will be displayed.)

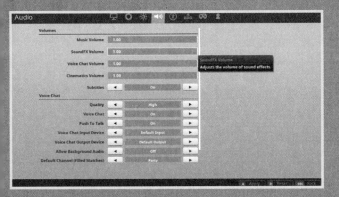

From the Audio submenu you're able to adjust the Music and Sound Effects volume, as well as the volume of the game's Voice Chat feature, for example. (Shown here on a PC.)

Either by clicking on the Game Menu icon in the top-right corner of the Lobby screen, or by clicking on the Social icon that's displayed in the top-left corner of the Lobby screen, you're able to access the Social menu. From here you can Add Friends, Send Invites (for people to join your Party), or use Voice Chat to communicate with other gamers.

If you're playing Fortnite: Battle Royale using a mouse and keyboard to control the action, access the Input submenu to tinker with and customize the key bindings associated with each command and action available during game play.

While viewing the Social menu, click on the gear-shaped icon to adjust your online privacy settings. From here, you can set your Online Status to "Online" or "Away," as well as your Party Privacy setting to "Public," "Friends Only," or "Private."

Anytime you want to play Fortnite: Battle Royale *or* Fortnite: Creative, *for example, and experience a match with other gamers as your partner or squad mates, send an Invite from the Social menu to specific online friends (one at a time). To do this, select the Party Up icon and then select the username for an online friend (assuming they're also online). Next, click on the Join Party option to send an Invite.*

To respond to an incoming Invite, return to the Lobby and make sure the Play tab is selected. Displayed to the right and left of your soldier (seen in the center of the screen) are three slots. Each has a "+" icon associated with it. If you see a yellow banner that includes an Invite, click on it to accept the invitation.

Fortnite: Battle Royale Offers Several Types of Challenges & Missions

Challenges were first introduced into *Fortnite: Battle Royale* during Season 3. At the start of Season 10, however, instead of Daily, Weekly, and Battle Pass Tier-based Challenges, Epic Games introduced **Missions,** in addition to other types of Challenges. Purchasing a Battle Pass is required to participate in most (but not all) Missions and Challenges.

By completing Missions, you'll earn Battle Pass Stars. These are used to unlock higher Battle Pass Tiers. For those gamers who don't purchase the current Battle Pass, certain Battle Pass Tiers also have Free Pass Challenges associated with them, but the prizes for completing these are not as exclusive or useful as what's offered for completing Battle Pass Missions and Challenges. No purchase is required to experience the Free Pass Challenges.

The good news is that if you do purchase a Battle Pass, you're able to unlock Free Pass Rewards, Battle Pass Rewards, and Mission-related Rewards by completing the various Challenges. Most Battle Pass Rewards are cosmetic items (such as Outfits) that have no impact on game play. They are items that become available from your soldier's Locker that allow you to customize their appearance.

Anytime you're in the Lobby, displayed on the left side of the screen (below the Social icon) is the season number, along with a summary of Challenges and/or the current Mission objective.

A Mission typically contains a set of "normal" Challenges, along with a separate set of more difficult "Prestige Challenges." These harder Prestige Challenges are designed for more experienced gamers. The Rewards earned depend on the number and level of difficulty of the Challenges completed during a Mission, for example.

A partial list of active Challenges can also be seen on the left side of the Island Map at any time while in the pre-deployment area or during a match. When you switch to the Island Map screen during a match, the match does not pause. The action still happens in real time around you. While you'll still hear what's going on, your view of the island will be blocked, so only access the Island Map when your soldier is in a safe place and there's little chance of an enemy sneaking up or launching an attack.

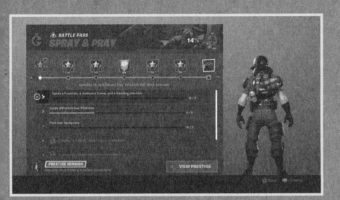

In order to unlock Prestige Mission Challenges, you'll first need to complete all normal Mission-oriented objectives, often in a specific order.

When in the Lobby, click on the Cycle Missions button to scroll through a summary of the different types of Challenges currently being offered (some of which are Mission related). Unlike other responsibilities you have during each match, Missions and Challenges do not need to be completed during a single match.

When you've purchased a Battle Pass, you'll discover that the Rewards that can be unlocked are more valuable and exclusive than prizes that can be unlocked by completing free Challenges. Meanwhile, once you've unlocked, purchased, or received certain Outfits, you can then complete Style-based challenges to unlock different styles for some of those Outfits.

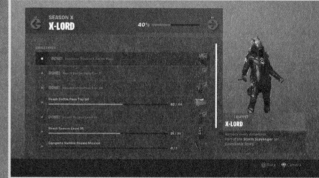

To discover what Style-based Challenges are currently available, click on the Challenges tab at the top of the Lobby screen, and then click on the Style tab.

Each of the Outfits that have unlockable Styles are displayed. Click on any one of them to reveal the Challenge(s) you'll need to complete to unlock one or more Styles associated with that Outfit. In some cases, the unlockable Style applies to an Outfit. Other Styles might apply to a Back Bling, Harvesting Tool, Glider design, or a Wrap design in the same Set as a specific Outfit.

Sometimes, when you purchase or unlock a specific Outfit, it comes with multiple Styles already unlocked. The Epic Outfit called Shade, for example, was sold in the Item Shop for 1,500 V-Bucks (about $15.00 US). It included three separate Styles that came unlocked as soon as the Outfit was purchased.

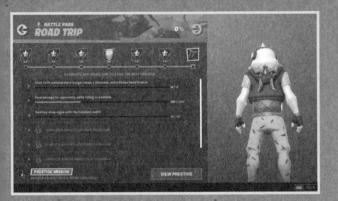

Anytime you click on the Challenges tab at the top of the Lobby screen, and then choose between an Event, Missions, or Style-based Challenge, click on the title and graphic for the Mission or Challenge to discover exactly what you'll need to do to complete it and see the Reward that will be unlocked once you're successful.

Keep in mind, at any given time, you can be working to complete multiple Challenges at once while you're participating in any matches within any game play mode of *Fortnite: Battle Royale*. Some Challenges, however, are game play mode-specific and can only be completed by competing in a Duos, Squads, or Team Rumble match, for example.

Even if you purchase a Battle Pass, you might not focus too much effort on completing Challenges or Missions, but if you adopt this strategy, your progress through the Battle Pass will be slow.

As you know, a Battle Pass is divided into 100 Tiers, all of which need to be unlocked before the current gaming season comes to an end.

Experience Points (XP) Allow You to Boost Your Season Level

Unlocking Battle Pass Tiers is different from boosting your Season Level. Simply by playing *Fortnite: Battle Royale*, you'll earn XP (Experience Points). You're awarded XP for defeating enemies, for completing certain Challenges, or just for staying alive and surviving during matches.

One item you can unlock as a prize for completing Challenges is an XP Boost, which will help to increase your Season Level. Your current Season Level is displayed on the left side of the Lobby screen, to the right of your soldier's Banner.

On the Lobby screen, directly below the Level indicator is a Level Meter. It shows you how much XP you still need to collect to progress to the next level.

As of Season 10, there are two types of XP Boosts available—a **Personal XP Boost** and a **Friend XP Boost**. Once you collect (or win) a Personal XP Boost, you'll earn extra XP at the end of every Solo *Fortnite: Battle Royale* match you complete.

A Friend XP Boost increases the amount of XP earned when you play a *Fortnite: Battle Royale* game play mode, such as Duos or Squads, that requires you to partner with other gamers. One of the fastest ways to boost your Season Level is to unlock or win XP Boosts, and then play *Fortnite: Battle Royale* with friends throughout the gaming season.

Important Concepts to Remember

- Season Level has no impact on your soldier's strength, speed, appearance, or tactical capabilities during a match.
- A Battle Pass will expire at the end of the current gaming season, whether or not you've unlocked all 100 Tiers.
- The Rewards you earn during each season are yours to keep forever. They get linked with your Epic Games account.
- Any XP Boosts that were activated during a specific season will expire at the end of that gaming season.
- Once a gaming season comes to an end, a new Battle Pass will become available starting on the first day of the next season. Each season's Battle Pass must be purchased separately.

- If you purchase a Battle Pass partway through a gaming season, any Tier-based objectives you've already completed will allow those Tiers to automatically unlock once the Battle Pass has been activated. To give yourself the best chance of unlocking all 100 Battle Pass Tiers during a specific season, it's best to purchase a Battle Pass as early in the season as possible.
- At the start of each new gaming season, once a new Battle Pass is purchased, you start again at Battle Pass Tier 1.
- The Outfits and related items (such as Back Bling designs, Glider designs, Harvesting Tool designs, Contrail designs, Wrap designs, and Emotes) you unlock that are related to a Battle Pass are exclusive to that gaming season and will not be reintroduced into the game later.

Think Strategy Before Each Match

Either before a match or at the start of one (while still aboard the Battle Bus), think carefully about what your overall strategy or objective during that match will be. If your goals are to stay alive as long as possible, gather a decent arsenal, be able to explore large portions of the island, and at the same time complete Challenges, for example, consider landing in a more remote area of the island where you're less apt to encounter enemy soldiers early on.

Also, before you reach the island and must contend with enemies and the storm, review the list of available Challenges carefully (from the

Lobby or Island Map) and determine what you need to accomplish, what items or weapons you'll need early on, which Outfit your soldier will need to wear (if applicable), and where on the island you're required to visit to complete the Challenge.

Instead of just challenging you to defeat enemies in combat, many Challenges require you to visit specific areas of the island during a single match, or find specific objects located on the island. If this is the case, choose your landing spot accordingly so you don't have to waste valuable time traveling across the island once the match kicks off.

Some challenges will require you to perform a range of tasks, not all of which will include engaging in combat. You may also be required to experience a specific game play mode (not Solo mode) to accomplish specific tasks, reach a specific Season Level, or stay alive longer than your opponents. In other words, you're rewarded for your survival skills.

For up-to-date descriptions of Challenges and Missions offered, starting from Season 3 to the current season, check out IGN's Fortnite Wiki Guide at: www.ign.com/wikis/fortnite/Weekly_Challenges#.

Keep in mind, some Challenges expire after a specific time period or at the end of a gaming season, while others roll over from season to season and remain available until they're completed.

SECTION 3

EVERYTHING YOU NEED TO KNOW ABOUT ACQUIRING A BATTLE PASS

As you know, a new Battle Pass becomes available at the start of each new *Fortnite: Battle Royale* gaming season. A Battle Pass must be purchased using V-Bucks, which cost real money.

To acquire a Battle Pass, from the Lobby, select the Battle Pass tab that's displayed along the top-center of the screen. The current Battle Pass screen will be displayed.

Many Types of Battle Pass Rewards Are Offered

Each Battle Pass is divided up into 100 Tiers. In the middle portion of the Battle Pass screen is a grid. Scroll through it to preview the prizes (Rewards) associated with each Battle Pass Tier. Shown here is the Battle Pass screen just after the Battle Bundle was purchased during Season 10. The first 25 Tiers have already been unlocked. You can also choose the View All Rewards option from the Battle Pass screen to preview all Battle Pass Rewards by type (as opposed to by Tier number).

The following is a summary of the various types of Battle Pass Tier Rewards. What's offered varies from season to season.

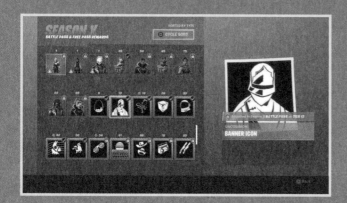

Banner Icons Graphics—These are graphics used to create your soldier's Banner. To create a Banner, access the Locker and choose the Banner slot displayed near the bottom-left corner of the screen.

Choose from the already unlocked Banner Icon graphics and select your Banner color. Your soldier's Banner is then displayed in several places when playing Fortnite: Battle Royale, including near the top-left corner of the Lobby, and on the Profile screen (which you can access by selecting the Career tab found at the top of the Lobby screen).

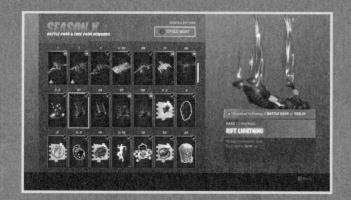

Contrail Designs—These are the animated graphics that shoot from a soldier's hands and/or feet during freefall from the Battle Bus at the start of a match. Contrail designs have no impact on your soldier's capabilities, freefall speed, or the navigational control you have over your soldier between when they leave the Battle Bus and when they land on the land.

Combo XP Boost—During some gaming seasons, you may be lucky enough to receive a Combo XP Boost as a reward. This one item gives you a 50 percent XP boost at the end of each Solo match you play, and a 60 percent XP boost at the end of each match you experience with friends for the duration of the current gaming season.

Dance Moves (Emotes)—These are individual dance moves your soldier can perform while in the pre-deployment area or during a match. Everyone who's controlling a soldier in close proximity to yours will see the dance move(s) your soldier performs. Quickly perform multiple dance moves one after another to create your own original choreography. There are hundreds of different Dance Moves available, and more are continuously being released either as Rewards or from the Item Shop. Shown here is a Dance Move called Blowing Bubbles.

Dance Moves are one of several types of Emotes available in *Fortnite: Battle Royale*. To perform a Dance Move, it must be one of the six Emotes selected from the Locker before a match. While in the pre-deployment area or during a match, access the Emotes menu to perform or use one of the Emotes (including Dance Moves) you've pre-selected. If you're controlling the game using a keyboard/mouse combat, instead of accessing the Emotes menu, simply press the keyboard key associated with the Emote you want to showcase.

Emotes, including Dance Moves, can be used to attract attention, taunt enemies, entertain yourself and others during slow periods of a match, or just for fun. Other types of Emotes include Emoticons, Spray Paint Tags, and Toys.

Emoticons (Emotes)—These are individual graphic icons that a soldier can toss into the air for all who are nearby to see. Emoticons can be used while in the pre-deployment area or anytime during a match. While there are many different Emoticons that can be unlocked and displayed, during any given match, you can only choose from six Emotes total.

Exclusive Outfits—Being able to unlock exclusive Outfits is the main reason why many gamers opt to purchase a Battle Pass. Each Battle Pass contains a selection of Outfits that are only available during that gaming season. Once a season ends, those Battle Pass Outfits won't be re-released in the future. Many of the Outfits introduced as part of a Battle Pass are based on a theme or plotline happening during that season. These typically become among the most popular Outfits offered in the game.

Friend XP Boosts—Unlocking these power-ups allow you to earn bonus XP each time you experience a match with one or more friends (such as when you play a Duos or Squads match, or one of the limited-time game play modes, such as a Team Rumble or Arena match).

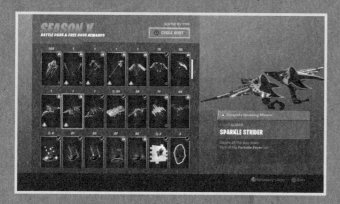

Glider Designs—These are exclusive Glider designs that are only available as Rewards for completing Missions and/or Challenges. Most of the Glider designers introduced as part of a Battle Pass are part of a theme-oriented set. A set often includes a matching Outfit, Glider design, Back Bling design, and Harvesting Tool design. Each item is available separately, either as Battle Pass Reward or from the Item Shop, for example.

Shown here in the Locker, each unlocked or purchased Glider design looks different, but they all function exactly the same way. Here are a few sample Glider designs. Which one you choose is a matter of personal preference.

Harvesting Tool Designs—Every soldier, during every match, has their own Harvesting Tool. This can be used as a close-range weapon. However, it'll take multiple whacks with a Harvesting Tool to cause any significant damage to an enemy. Using a Harvesting Tool as a weapon is no match against any other type of weapon.

A Harvesting Tool is more commonly used to smash objects on the island in order to collect resources—wood, stone (brick), or metal, or to clear a pathway for your soldier. Resources are used for building. Smash anything made of wood (such as trees, pallets, or the walls of some structures) to collect wood. Smash piles of stone or anything made of brick to collect stone. To collect metal, use the Harvesting tool to smash anything made out of metal, such as broken-down vehicles, machinery, or kitchen appliances within homes.

At the very start of a match, when your soldier first lands on the island, the only item they'll have in their possession is their trusty Harvesting Tool. This soldier is wearing the Rare-ranked Breakpoint Outfit and using the Rare-ranked Fated Frame Harvesting tool. His Back Bling design is the Rare-rated Signal Jammer. Each of these items is from a different set. From the Locker, you can easily mix and match items to give your soldier a unique appearance.

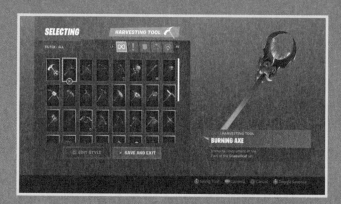

Loading Screen Graphics—This is the graphic you see when you launch Fortnite and the game is loading, for example. The Loading Screen Graphic has no impact on game play whatsoever.

Music Tracks—During gameplay, background music is continuously played. By collecting different Music Tracks (and selecting one from the Locker), you're able to decide what music you'll hear while playing Fortnite: Battle Royale. Many gamers, however, opt to turn off the music altogether, and at the same time turn up the volume of the game's sound effects. Sound effects play a vital role in the game. Adjusting the music and sound effect levels can be done by accessing the Settings menu and selecting the Audio submenu.

Here's a selection of unlocked Harvesting Tool designs from the soldier's Locker (accessed prior to a match). This item is carried by your soldier at all times and cannot be dropped. While each Harvesting Tool design may look different, all Harvesting Tools function exactly the same way—regardless of their size or appearance.

Outfit Styles—In addition to hundreds of unique Outfits you can unlock, receive, or purchase when playing Fortnite: Battle Royale, many of the newer Outfits can be customized by unlocking and using Outfit Styles. Not all Outfits have Styles associated with them. Styles can be won as prizes for completing Battle Pass Challenges, Missions, or Style Challenges. Some Styles can be purchased from the Item Shop. Outfit Styles can only be used if you've already purchased, received, or unlocked the Outfit the Style is compatible with. Shown here are two Styles that could be unlocked during Season 10 for the Ultima Knight Outfit.

Once you've acquired a compatible Outfit and have unlocked, received, or purchased separate Styles for it, return to the Locker, select a compatible Outfit, and then choose one of the unlocked Styles that are displayed to customize the appearance of that Outfit. You can further customize the appearance of your soldier by choosing their Back Bling design and Harvesting Tool design, for example.

Personal XP Boosts—As you play Fortnite: Battle Royale, once a Personal XP Boost has been collected and activated, you'll receive bonus XP at the end of each Solo match during the current gaming season. XP is used to increase your Season Level as a gamer. Unlocking one 10 percent Personal XP Boost (shown here), for example, will give you a 10 percent XP bonus at the end of each Solo match for the duration of the gaming season.

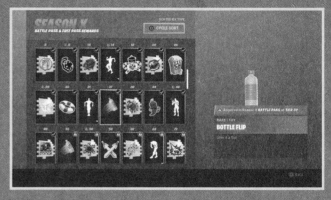

Spray Paint Tags (Emotes)–These are another type of Emote available within Fortnite: Battle Royale. Once you've unlocked one or more Spray Paint Tags, select up to six of them prior to a match from the Locker. While in the pre-deployment area or anytime during a match, your soldier can than spray paint a specific Spray Paint Tag design onto any flat surface, such as the wall or floor of a building, structure, or fortress.

Toys (Emotes)–These are another type of Emote that can be added to your soldier's Emotes menu once they're individually unlocked. Toys are interactive items you're able to use while exploring the island. For example, there are basketballs, beach balls, flying discs, and water bottles that can be played with.

There are many different Spray Paint Tags that can be unlocked, received, or acquired. By pre-selecting two or three of them from the Locker to be part of your soldier's Emotes Menu during a match, you're then able to mix and match Spray Paint Tag designs to create colorful graffiti on the island. Only Spray Paint Tags that have been unlocked and stored within your soldier's Locker are available to choose from.

During Season 10, for example, a water bottle (Bottle Flip) Toy could be acquired by unlocking Battle Pass Tier 37. During a match, toss the water bottle toward the ground and try to make it land upright (as opposed to on its side). This is a fun way to spend time during a match, but it has no impact on game play whatsoever, except that it can distract you from incoming surprise attacks.

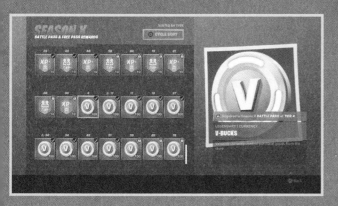

V-Buck Bundles—Normally, V-Bucks need to be purchased in bundles of 1,000, 2,800, 5,000, or 13,500 from the Store. However, it's also possible to unlock bundles of 100 V-Bucks as rewards for completing Missions and Challenges. V-Bucks are then used to make purchases from the Item Shop.

Virtual Pets—These are adorable creatures that can be carried within special backpacks that your soldier then wears during a match. While the virtual pets are interactive, they have no impact whatsoever on game play or your soldier's tactical capabilities. Each gaming season, at least two or three different virtual pets are made available as Rewards for unlocking Battle Pass Tiers. Virtual Pets are not typically sold within the Item Shop.

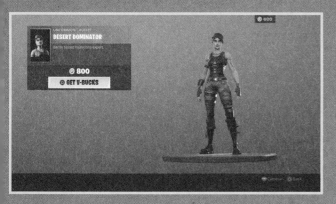

The least expensive item typically sold within the Item Shop is a specific Wrap for 300 V-Bucks (approximately $3.00 US). Depending on how an Outfit is categorized (Common, Uncommon, Rare, Epic, or Legendary), the cost of one Outfit from the Item Shop will be between 500 and 2,000 V-Bucks (or between $5.00 and $20.00 US). Shown here is the Uncommon Desert Dominator Outfit that's priced at 800 V-Bucks (about $8.00 US). A Harvesting Tool or Glider design, for example, might cost between 500 and 800 V-Bucks each (which equates to between $5.00 and $8.00 US).

During Season 10, for example, Kitsune was a feline virtual pet that was associated with Tier 28. The Kitsune (Snowstorm) Style for the pet could be acquired by unlocking Tier 45 during Season 10.

In the past, other virtual pets introduced into the game included: Bonesy (a dog), Camo (a lizard), Dodger (a fox), Kyo (a robotic pet), and Woodsy (a dog).

Shown here is Camo, a virtual pet lizard.

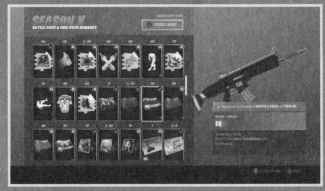

Wraps—These are special graphic designs used to decorate specific types of weapons and items found on the island. Some Wraps are animated. Within your soldier's Locker, there are several different Wrap slots. Each is used to select an unlocked Wrap for a specific type of weapon or item. There are separate Wrap slots for vehicles, Assault Rifles, Shotguns, SMGs, Sniper Rifles, Pistols, and Miscellaneous Items, for example. After Wraps are received, purchased, or unlocked, you can access them from the Locker.

Once a virtual pet is unlocked, it gets stored within your soldier's Locker and is considered a type of Back Bling design. It can be seen on your soldier's back throughout each match that it's worn. During this match, the soldier was wearing the Carbon Commando Outfit along with the Dodger virtual pet (Back Bling) on his back.

XP—As a reward for completing some Mission-based Challenges, for example, you'll sometimes receive a specific amount of XP on a one-time basis at the end of a match as a Reward. The number of XP could between 500 and 5,000. There's also a special type of Personal XP Boost Reward (shown here) that gives you Bonus XP at the start of the next gaming season.

How to Purchase a Battle Pass

If you have not yet purchased a Battle Pass during the current gaming season, from the Lobby, select the Battle Pass tab at the top of the screen, and then from the Battle Pass screen, choose the Purchase option (found near the bottom-left corner of the screen).

For 2,800 V-Bucks (approximately $28.00 US), you can purchase a Battle Bundle. This unlocks the current season's Battle Pass, and at the same time, instantly unlocks the first 25 Battle Pass Tiers, so you're awarded those Tier-based Rewards immediately, without having to complete any Missions or Challenges.

If you don't have enough V-Bucks, be sure to visit the Store before you attempt to purchase a Battle Pass or Battle Pass Bundle.

There are two purchase options for each Battle Pass. Make your choice from this menu screen.

A basic Battle Pass (shown here for Season 10) activates the current Battle Pass immediately. It's available for 950 V-Bucks, which is equivalent to about $9.50 US.

In addition to purchasing a Battle Pass (or Battle Pass Bundle) for yourself, from the Battle Pass screen, you have the option to purchase either a Battle Pass or Battle Pass Bundle for an online friend. To do this, from the Battle Pass screen, select the Gift Battle Pass option (found near the bottom-center of the screen).

From the Select Recipients screen, one at a time, choose which online friend(s) you want to buy a Battle Pass or Battle Pass Bundle for as a gift. You'll need to spend V-Bucks (which cost real money) to give these gifts to other people.

Also from the Battle Pass screen, if you select the View All Rewards option, a separate screen is displayed that allows you to preview each of the Rewards (prizes) offered in conjunction with each of the 100 Tiers associated with that Battle Pass. Displayed directly above each slot is the Tier Number the Reward is associated with. Shown here, the slot in the top-left corner of the screen is displayed. This shows the X-Lord Outfit, which was the prize associated with unlocking Tier 1 during Season 10.

The slot to the right of the X-Lord Outfit shows the Catalyst Outfit, which was also a Reward for unlocking Tier 1 of Season 10. Along the top row of slots on this screen, you can see the five other exclusive Outfits that were offered as Rewards associated with Tier 23 (Tilted Teknique), Tier 47 (Yond3R), Tier 70 (Sparkle Supreme), Tier 87 (Eternal Voyager), and Tier 100 (Ultimate Knight) during Season 10. During the gaming season you're about to experience, this selection of Outfits and what Tier they're associated with will be different.

Regardless of the gaming season, you can be sure that the Tier 100 Reward will always be an ultra-exclusive, Legendary Outfit. Ultimate Knight (from Season 10) is shown here. If you did not unlock this Outfit by the end of Season 10, it will never again be offered within Fortnite: Battle Royale.

If after reading this strategy guide you still have some questions about how Battle Passes work, check out the Battle Pass Help feature within the game. To access it, select the Battle Pass tab from the Lobby. Next, select the About Battle Pass option displayed near the bottom-right corner of the Battle Pass screen. When the How Does It Work? screen appears, select the Help option that's displayed near the bottom-right corner of the screen.

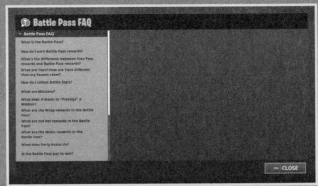

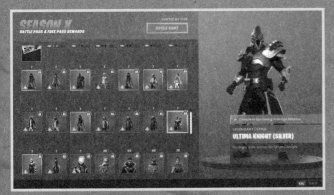

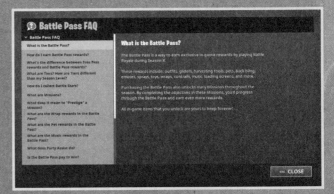

As you scroll down within the Battle Pass and Free Pass Rewards screen for the current gaming season, after viewing the slots associated with the Outfit Rewards, you can see the slots associated with the exclusive Back Bling design Rewards, followed by the Harvesting Tool design Rewards, the Contrail design Rewards, the Emoticon Rewards, the Wrap Rewards, the Loading Screen Graphic Rewards, the Outfit Style Rewards, the Banner Icon Rewards, the XP Boost Rewards, and the V-Buck Bundle Rewards, for example.

Once you've accessed this Battle Pass FAQ (Frequently Asked Questions) screen, scroll down and read the most commonly asked questions related to Battle Passes on the left side of the screen, and then read the answer to each of those questions (provided by Epic Games) on the right side of the screen (once you highlight and select a question).

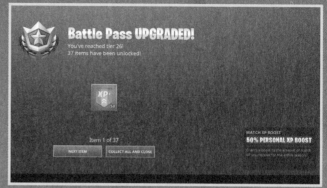

If you purchased a Battle Pass Bundle, the Outfits and other items associated with the first 25 Tiers of the current season's Battle Pass are unlocked and displayed one at a time. Select the Next Item option to view the next Reward, see a description for what it is (and what it does), and add it to your soldier's Locker. Alternatively, to save time, select the Collect All and Close option.

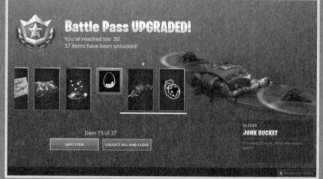

When applicable, Outfits or other items will be placed in the appropriate section of your soldier's Locker upon getting unlocked. Shown here is the X-Lord Outfit being unlocked (during Season 10).

Shown here is a Glider design and Contrail design also being unlocked upon purchasing a Battle Bundle.

How to Purchase and Unlock Battle Pass Tiers

Shown here, five Tiers are about to be purchased and unlocked. One of the Rewards will be a Dance Move. The cost will be 750 V-Bucks (150 V-Bucks times five.)

If you purchased just the Battle Pass, when you're returned to the Battle Pass screen, you'll likely see that none of the Tiers have yet been unlocked. However, if you purchased the Battle Bundle option, you'll discover the first 25 Tiers of the current season's Battle Pass have been unlocked. At this point, you can start playing Fortnite: Battle Royale, complete the Missions and Challenges, and receive the applicable Rewards. Alternatively, from the Battle Pass screen, select the Buy Tiers option, and then using 150 V-Bucks each (approximately $1.50 US), purchase and unlock one Tier at a time to immediately receive the Reward associated with that Tier.

As soon as an Outfit has been received as a Reward and unlocked, you can immediately access it from your soldier's Locker. Shown here is the X-Lord Outfit being selected from the Locker before a match.

Upon selecting the Buy Tiers option, this Purchase Tier screen is displayed. Select how many Tiers you want to purchase and unlock at once. Each time you increase the number of Tiers to Unlock, the Rewards associated with those Tiers is displayed, so you can see the prizes you'll receive upon making the purchase. Shown here, just one Tier is selected, and the Reward is a bundle of 100 V-Bucks. Spending 150 V-Bucks to unlock just 100 V-Bucks is not a good deal. You'll come out 50 V-Bucks behind, but you will advance one Tier in the Battle Pass without doing any work. In this case, you might want to complete a Mission or Challenge(s) to acquire more Battle Stars and use them to unlock the Tier, so you don't have to pay to unlock it.

Assuming you've purchased a Battle Pass (or in this case a Battle Pass Bundle) near the start of a new season, as soon as the Battle Pass is active, return to the Lobby to begin playing Fortnite: Battle Royale. *Before choosing a game play mode, consider visiting the Locker to customize the appearance of your soldier. You might also want to access the game's Settings menu to tweak the various options to customize your game play experience and the control you'll have over the game. When you're ready, select a game play mode (Solo is shown here), and then choose the Play option to enter a match.*

SECTION 4

STRATEGIES FOR WORKING YOUR WAY THROUGH THE 100 BATTLE PASS TIERS

During past gaming seasons, there were specific Tier-based Challenges you needed to complete to directly unlock one Battle Pass Tier at a time. There were also separate Daily, Weekly, and Style Challenges, as well as Free Pass Challenges. This changed somewhat at the start of Season 10, when Missions were introduced into the game.

Now, completing Missions and Challenges allow you to earn Battle Stars that automatically get redeemed to unlock Battle Pass Tiers as you progress throughout a gaming season. Battle Stars are earned based on the number of Challenges you complete.

A Mission is a set of normal Challenges. It also sometimes includes a set of Prestige Challenges that you can complete once you've completed the Mission's Normal Challenges. Doing this allows you to earn additional Rewards.

Some Missions require you to experience a specific game play mode and accomplish specific tasks while playing matches in that game play mode. Recently, Epic Games has put a lot of emphasis on rewarding gamers for playing Duos, Squads, or limited-time Team Rumble or Arena matches.

To discover what Challenges are currently available to you, look for a summary of individual Challenges listed on the left side of the Lobby screen. From the Lobby screen, select the Challenges tab to view a more detailed listing of Missions and Challenges. A list of currently available Missions and Challenges can also be found on the right side of the Island Map screen.

It's best to preview available Challenges, and what's required to complete them, *before* starting a match. This allows you to begin planning your strategies early on.

Mission- and Challenge-Related Questions That'll Help You Prepare

Since there are so many different types of Missions and Challenges available to complete at any given time (and new ones are released weekly), once you decide to begin working your way through a specific Mission or Challenge, ask yourself the following series of questions to help improve your chances of success and save time completing the required tasks.

1. Which game play mode do you need to choose to complete a specific Mission or Challenge?
2. Do you need to select a specific Outfit for your soldier to wear prior to a match to complete a Mission or Challenge? For example, in one Challenge during Season 10, a gamer was required to have their soldier wear the X-Lord Outfit and build 200 structures while playing the Team Rumble game play mode.
3. To complete the objective(s), will you need to visit one or more specific points of interest (locations) on the island during a match? If so, where is the best place to land to help you reach those destinations the fastest?
4. Are specific weapons or items required to complete the Mission or Challenge objectives? If so, where will you find and acquire those weapons and/or items? This too should impact where you choose to land at the start of a match.

5. What is the specific objective? Do you need to defeat a certain number of enemies or inflict a specific amount of damage using a specific weapon, item, vehicle, or tool? For example, a Challenge might require you to deal a specific amount of damage to opponents during a single match using any weapon or item, but another Challenge might require you to eliminate an enemy using a specific type of weapon or explosive.

6. Is there a time limit associated with the Mission or Challenge? Does the specific Mission or Challenge expire at the end of a day or week, or the end of a gaming season, whether or not it's been completed? Most Style-based Challenges, for example, never expire, and roll over from gaming season to gaming season until they're completed.

7. Will you need to work with a partner or squad mates to complete one or more specific objectives? If so, how and when will you communicate with those other gamers to coordinate your efforts?

8. Have you memorized the multiple Challenges associated with a Match, so you don't have to waste time reviewing what's required? For example, the objective may be to participate in five Team Rumble matches and achieve at least one elimination per match. Another objective might be to win three Team Rumble matches. In this case, since a Team Rumble match divides the 100 gamers into two teams, you simply need to be on the winning team three times.

9. What normal game play activities will also help you complete Missions or Challenges? In some cases, a Challenge might require you to simply open a specific number of chests during a single match or open a specific number of Supply Drops during the gaming season. Likewise, a Challenge might include defeating one or more enemies using a long-range weapon (such as a Sniper Rifle) from at least 100 meters away. This is something you're likely to do as part of your quest to achieve #1 Victory Royale during a match.

10. What new, season-specific weapons, items, vehicles, locations, or themes relate to the Mission or Challenge(s) at hand? Each season has a different storyline that unfolds which impacts the terrain on the island, for example. If a Challenge requires you to experience something that's brand new in a gaming season, before trying to complete the Challenge or Mission (and survive during an actual match), get acquainted with what's new by visiting Playground mode. Gain experience and learn your way around the newer points of interest, or boost your competency using new weapons or items, before jumping into an actual match.

Remember, many types of Missions and Challenges don't require you to defeat lots of enemies. In some cases, you only need to inflict a specific amount of damage to them (potentially using a specific type of weapon). Other Challenges that require you to open Chests, Supply Drops, use Vending Machines, build structures, or simply visit specific locations, for example, have nothing whatsoever to do with combat.

Some Missions and Objectives don't specify which *Fortnite: Battle Royale* game play mode you need to experience to complete the required tasks. You'll discover it's often easier to complete certain challenges by playing a limited-time Team Rumble match (as opposed to a Solo, Duos, or Squads match) since your soldier can easily respawn numerous times during a match, and you always have many teammates available to watch your back during intense combat situations.

In some cases, even though it's not specifically required, you might benefit from working with three other squad mates during a Squads match to complete specific Missions or Challenges, since you'll have the ability to communicate in real-time during matches, coordinate your efforts, and help each other out.

How to Earn Battle Stars

Starting with Season 10, the two ways to unlock Battle Pass Tiers (once you've purchased a Battle Pass) are to complete Mission Challenges and other Challenges that offer Battle Stars as a Reward, or to pay 150 V-Bucks per Tier that you want to unlock (without having to do any work). Thus, it's a good strategy to focus on Missions and Challenges that allow you to receive Battle Stars (as opposed to other Rewards).

From the Lobby, select the Challenges tab at the top of the screen to scroll through all of the current Missions and Challenges available.

Select the Event or Mission tab near the top-center of the screen, and then scroll to the right to view the title and graphic for each Mission or Challenge that's currently available. Notice that some displayed Missions don't begin for a few days or weeks. They're simply previewed and include a timer showing when they'll be unlocked.

Choose one Mission or Challenge that's displayed to view a detailed description of the Rewards and specific Challenges you need to complete. When you select a Mission, it will list a handful of different Challenges, each with its own Reward. You do not need to complete all of the Challenges within a Mission to receive Battle Stars. You'll receive a Reward for each individual Mission Challenge you complete, as soon as you complete it.

If your goal is to unlock Battle Pass Tiers, choose Missions that offer Battle Stars as a Reward. As you can see here, the Road Trip Mission screen is displayed. The Reward for completing the first, second, third, fifth, and sixth Challenge is 10 Battle Stars each. In this case, to unlock all of the normal Challenges within this Mission, you first need to complete the first three. As you progress, you can unlock the remaining four normal missions, and then unlock the Prestige missions.

As you can see, the Rewards offered for some Mission Challenges include Outfit Styles or Emotes, as opposed to Battle Stars. These are great for expanding what's available in your soldier's Locker when it comes to customizing the appearance of your soldier, but without earning Battle Stars, you can't unlock Battle Pass Tiers. Shown here is the Season 10 Mission, called Level-Headed. It offers no Battle Stars for completing Challenges.

Click on the Back button to exit out of the Mission description screen. Return to the Battle Pass screen by clicking on the Battle Pass tab that's displayed near the top-center of the screen. Near the top-right corner of the Battle Pass Reward chart, you'll see the most recent Tier you've unlocked (in this case it's Tier 53). To the immediate left of the Tier indicator is an orange banner that displays how many Battle Stars you've collected, and how many are required to unlock the next Tier. In this case, eight out of 10 more Battle Stars must be collected to unlock Tier 54.

Each week during a gaming season, new Missions are unlocked. Look for Missions that clearly offer multiple bundles of Battle Stars as Rewards so you can continuously unlock Battle Pass Tiers.

Once you determine a specific Mission offers multiple Challenges that offer Battle Stars as a Reward, read the Challenge objectives carefully and determine if based on your gaming skills, you're capable of completing those Challenges.

For example, during Season 10, the Rumble Royale Mission included seven normal Challenges and seven Prestige Challenges. The first three Challenge objectives for the Rumble Royale Mission included:

- Play matches of Team Rumble with at least one elimination. As you can see from the Mission description screen, to receive the 10 Battle Stars for completing this objective, you needed to participate in five Team Rumble missions and defeat at least one enemy during each.

- Win a match of Team Rumble. To receive the 10 Battle Stars associated with this Challenge, you needed to be on the winning team for three Team Rumble matches, but you did not need to win three in a row.

- Assist teammates with eliminations in Team Rumble. To achieve this objective and receive 10 Battle Stars, you needed to help eliminate 20 enemies. This could be done over the course of as many separate Team Rumble matches as necessary. Notice that the objective was to "assist" with an enemy elimination. This means you just need to inflict damage on enemies (and have a teammate eliminate them). You don't necessarily need to defeat the enemies yourself.

Especially if you're a newb, choose Mission Challenges that you're confident you can complete quickly, based on your skill level and experience. Keep in mind, you can complete one or two Challenges from one Mission, and then switch your focus to Challenges from another Mission, or attempt to complete Challenges from several missions at the same time.

The Missions and Challenges showcased in this guide are from Season 10. When you experience *Fortnite: Battle Royale*, the selection of Missions and Challenges, as well as the Rewards offered will all be different. The goal, however, remains to collect Battle Stars by completing Challenges in order to unlock Battle Pass Tiers.

At least during Season 10, the Event and Style-based Missions and Challenges did not allow you to earn Battle Stars. Instead, other Rewards were offered. After choosing the Challenges tab, if you select the Style option, you'll see a selection of Outfits that have Styles available that can be unlocked by completing Challenges. Unless you have already purchased or unlocked the Outfit itself (and it's accessible from your soldier's Locker), there's no point in completing Challenges for Styles you can't use.

Focus your attention and efforts on Style-related Challenges that will allow you to unlock Styles for some of your favorite Outfits that you already have purchased or unlocked. As you can see, these Challenges do not expire, so in this case, you can unlock Styles related to the Calamity, Ragnarok, and Drift Outfits, which were Outfits released as far back as Season 5.

Need Help? Take Advantage of Party Assist

Anytime you're experiencing a Duos, Squads, or team-based gaming mode, you have the ability to use *Fortnite: Battle Royale's* "Party Assist" feature to help you complete Missions and Challenges faster, with the help of your friends.

For this to work to your advantage, you need to communicate with your partner or squad mates and have them agree to help you achieve specific objectives during matches you participate in together.

To turn on the Party Assist feature for a specific Challenge, open a Mission description screen, and the select a specific Challenge.

Notice that a Party Assist button appears for that Challenge. Click on this button to activate the feature. You can only turn on Party Assist for one Challenge at a time, so choose Challenges that are more difficult and that you don't have the patience or gaming skills to complete yourself.

Additional Strategies for Completing Missions and Challenges

Anytime you're faced with a challenge that is like a scavenger hunt and that requires you to find multiple items or objects, chances are you won't be able to travel to each location during one match. You may find it easier to participate in a Team Rumble match (so your soldier can easily respawn) and focus on trying to reach the locations as quickly as possible, using a vehicle, if available.

If you need to visit specific points of interest on the island that are labeled on the Island Map, you can easily check the Island Map to determine where you need to go and the quickest way to get there. However, if you're looking for an object that's not labeled on the map, such as a Durr Burger Head (shown here), one option is to randomly explore the map until you find it. It's best to do this in Playground mode. Then, once you locate the item, enter into a regular match and revisit the location to access the object.

Another option for finding objects on the island is to visit YouTube (www.YouTube.com) and within the Search field, type the season number, followed by the name of Mission you're trying to complete. For example, type "Fortnite Season 10 Road Trip," to discover tutorial videos that explain where to find exactly what you're looking for and the quickest way to reach the locations where you'll find those objects. Shown here is a YouTube video from TheLlamaSir (www.youtube.com/user/TheLlamaSir) that demonstrates exactly how to complete the Season 10 Road Trip Mission, for example.

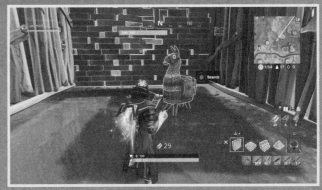

Regardless of the Challenge you're trying to pursue, chances are you'll need to defend your soldier against enemy attacks. The best way to build up a strong arsenal is to open chests, Loot Llamas, Supply Drops, and Loot Carriers (drones). The best ammo, especially Rockets, are typically found in Ammo Boxes, as opposed to lying on the ground, out in the open.

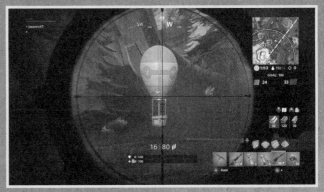

When possible, take advantage of what's offered by Vending Machines to strengthen your arsenal with more powerful and rare weapons.

Sometimes, the easiest way to eliminate an enemy is from a distance using any weapon with a scope, such as a Sniper Rifle. From far away and while hidden, target your weapon on an object, such as a chest or Supply Drop, that you know an enemy will approach. As soon as the enemy steps into your weapon's targeting crosshairs or viewfinder, shoot them. This is much easier than trying to target a fast-moving enemy from a distance, especially if the weapon you're using has a very small Magazine (Mag) and a long Reload time.

As you work toward unlocking the Tiers in a Battle Pass, some of the Challenges will require you to eliminate enemies from the match. Sometimes using a specific weapon is required. Often, however, weapon selection will be at your discretion, so choose the weapon you have the most accuracy using in combat.

Defeating enemies is always easier if you have a height advantage over your opponent. In a close-range firefight, achieving a height advantage might mean jumping up onto an object or shooting at your enemy on the first floor of a structure from the second floor.

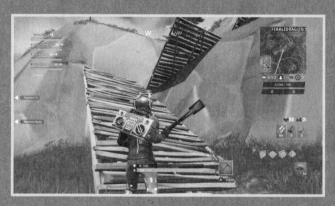

You also have the ability to quickly build a ramp using wood, stone, or metal in almost any location on the island to achieve a height advantage. Ramps can also be used to quickly reach the top of a building, structure, or hill, for example.

When using a long-range weapon, you can be on the roof of a building, or the top of a hill or mountain and shoot at an enemy on ground level, for example.

Keep in mind, however, if you build a very tall ramp, an enemy can simply shoot at one of the bottom tiles of the ramp and the whole thing will come crashing down. If your soldier is more than three levels off the ground, they'll likely perish from the fall unless they quickly deploy a Glider item or another tool to go airborne.

Building bridges between two structures is one way to get from one to the other quickly, while maintaining a height advantage.

Standing on the top of a hill and shooting down at a target also gives your soldier a height advantage. In this case, a Supply Drop just landed and enemy soldiers will soon be approaching it. As soon as one of the enemies reaches the Supply Drop, the soldier on the hill can shoot them from above.

Once you decide where you need to go on the island, whether you're playing a Solo, Duos, or Squads match, access the Island Map and place a Marker at your desired destination. Your enemies will not be able to see any Markers you place, but you, along with your allies, will be able to see it from great distances, plus be able to quickly determine how far away you are based on your current location on the island. Even in Solo mode, Markers make finding your way around the island easier, especially if you know where you're headed and it's a far distance from your current location.

In general, the best weapons, loot, and tools can typically be found within the labeled points of interest on the Island Map. These also tend to be the most popular locations, so your chances of encountering enemies increases dramatically. Located on the outskirts of virtually every labeled point of interest, however, is at least one structure, building, or unlabeled area where you're virtually guaranteed to find a few weapons, ammo, Health/Shield replenishment items, and/or loot items if you're the first one to visit that area. At the start of a match, this soldier landed on the roof of a small shack located on a hill outside of what was Tilted Town during Season 10. Within this structure was a chest filled with weapons and ammo.

Visiting one or more of the unlabeled areas before stepping into the heart of a popular point of interest allows you to build a more powerful arsenal, and potentially activate or boost your soldier's Shields, so when you do ultimately encounter enemies, you'll be more heavily armed and better prepared. This gas station is located on the outskirts of what was Pleasant Park during Season 10. It too offered weapons and ammo to the first person to enter the structure and grab what was available.

At any given time, there are many different Missions and Challenges you can be working to complete during a single match. If one of the Challenges requires you to find and destroy several of a specific item (such as Stop Signs) to complete the objective, when you decide this is the Challenge you want to focus on, at the start of a Mission think carefully about where on the island you're most apt to find Stop Signs. (Hint: It's within the urban areas and small town-like areas on the island.) Choose your landing location accordingly.

Pleasant Park (during Season 10) was a suburban neighborhood with a few houses located in close proximity. This area's streets contained multiple Stop Signs in close proximity. Visiting here would allow you to complete the Challenge requiring you to destroy multiple Stop Signs much faster.

During Season 10, for example, one of the Challenges (which was part of the Road Trip Mission) was to find and destroy 10 Stop Signs while wearing the Catalyst Outfit. Due to the expansion and movement of the storm, being able to reach enough locations on the island during a single match to destroy enough Stop Signs was not possible. This is a Challenge that needed to be completed over the course of

multiple Solo, Duos, Squads, or Team Rumble matches, so plan accordingly to receive the available 10 Battle Star Rewards.

Another Challenge might require you to open at least one chest located in several different labeled points of interest on the map. Depending on where you land, this Challenge could potentially be completed during a single match, especially if you participate in a Team Rumble match where you can roam on your team's half of the island during the early stages of the match with little chance of encountering enemies. At the start of a match, check out the Island Map and consider a travel route that could take you through multiple points of interest quickly, knowing that your goal is to simply open a chest in each location and then move on.

There may be Challenges that require you to visit two labeled points of interest that are located on opposite sides of the island. To accomplish this, you'll probably need to use a vehicle. Alternatively, participate in a Team Rumble–type match that allows you to get eliminated from a match and then respawn within seconds in a totally different (albeit) random location that the storm has not reached yet. Doing this intentionally increases your chances of being able to reach locations that are otherwise far apart.

Don't forget that some Challenges require you to use specific items to accomplish specific tasks. For example, if your objective is to use Spray Paint Tags on three different locations during a match, before starting that match, you'll need to access the Locker and load up at least one of the six Emote slots with unlocked Spray Paint Tags, since these can't be accessed from the Locker during a match unless they've already been added to the Emotes menu.

Especially if you're a newb, or you haven't yet mastered the art of using weapons to defeat enemies, as you begin working your way through the Battle Pass Tiers, read the Challenge requirements for all available Missions first, and then choose the easiest ones that allow you to receive 10 Battle Stars each, without having to engage in combat. If you focus on these Challenges first, within one to three days, you should be able to make your way at least through Tier 40 or Tier 50 of the current season's Battle Pass. You'll likely then have plenty of time remaining in the gaming season to complete the rest of the more difficult Challenges.

When approaching any building or structure and you notice the door has already been opened, this means someone has been inside—and may still be there. Instead of walking directly through the door, stand to the side and peek inside, or perhaps toss a few explosive weapons through the door to clear your path, in case an enemy is lurking inside waiting for you.

As you approach a structure, consider tiptoeing during your approach to make as little noise as possible, and then peeking through a window to see if you spot an enemy inside. If you do, consider shooting them directly through the window.

Zipline Travel Can Help You Complete Some Challenges Faster

Some *Fortnite: Battle Royale* gaming seasons offer a more diverse selection of vehicles than others. During Season 10, for example, Quadcrashers and Ballers were vaulted, and Driftboards (Hoverboards) remained available on the island but were scarce.

Slipstreams were also vaulted, but a network of Ziplines remained on the island as a viable transportation method for your soldier. (Any of these other vehicles, or brand new vehicles, could be introduced back into the game at any time.)

While a particular Challenge might require you to travel via Zipline to accomplish a specific objective, at almost any time you're able to use the island's Zipline network to travel potentially far distances faster than walking or running.

Inside the Outposts (red buildings) usually located on one end of a Zipline route, you'll often find a cheat, and/or weapons, items, and ammo lying on the ground. These Outposts are not typically within labeled points of interest on the map, but they're a great place to stop and replenish or expand your soldier's arsenal.

Ziplines are one way to get around certain parts of the island. The drawback to using them is that you can't determine exactly where you want to go. Your soldier has to travel along one of the established Zipline routes. On the plus side, your soldier can travel in either direction along a Zipline, and using your navigational controls, you can switch directions or stop while traveling along a Zipline. It's also possible to shoot weapons and use items while travel via Zipline. To improve your aim, stop moving, shoot, and then continue traveling toward the end of the Zipline route. Yes, enemy soldiers can shoot at your soldier while they're traveling along a Zipline.

While traveling along a Zipline, press the Jump button on your controller or keyboard to leap off of the Zipline at any point before the starting or ending point of the route. Keep in mind, if the Zipline is high off the ground, you could perish by crash landing on the ground. Also, two opposing soldiers can travel in the same or opposite directions simultaneously on a single Zipline. However, if two soldiers crash, both will fall from the Zipline to the ground, so avoid potentially fatal crashes.

Anytime a soldier builds a ramp, bridge, or structure, for example, another soldier can come along and destroy those objects. In fact, most buildings and structures found on the island can be destroyed using repetitive gunfire, explosives, or even a soldier's Harvesting Tool. Keep in mind, however, that the metal posts used to create Ziplines cannot be damaged or destroyed, so don't bother trying to damage this transportation option while exploring the island.

SECTION 5

FORTNITE: BATTLE ROYALE
RESOURCES

On any of the popular gaming-related streaming services, within the Search field, enter the phrase *"Fortnite: Battle Royale,"* to discover many game-related channels, live streams, and prerecorded videos that'll help you become a better player and complete each of the Missions offered during the latest gaming season.

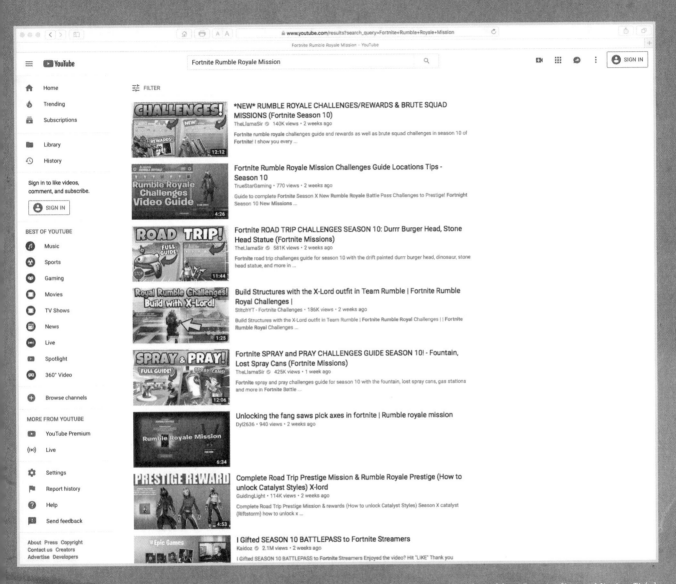

If you need help completing a specific Mission's Challenges, within the Search field, enter something like, "Fortnite [Insert Mission Title] Mission," to find a tutorial that'll help you complete that Mission. For example, type "Fortnite Rumble Royale Mission" to find video tutorials that'll help you complete the Challenges within that one Mission.

To set up a free account and watch the videos and live streams offered on the most popular gaming-related services, visit:

- **Facebook Watch**—www.facebook.com/watch
- **Mixer**—https://mixer.com/browse/games/70323/fortnite
- **Twitch.tv**—www.twitch.tv/directory/game/Fortnite
- **YouTube**—www.youtube.com

Also, be sure to check out these other online resources related to *Fortnite: Battle Royale*:

WEBSITE OR YOUTUBE CHANNEL NAME	DESCRIPTION	URL
Best *Fortnite* Settings	Discover the custom game settings used by some of the world's top-rated *Fortnite: Battle Royale* players.	www.bestfortnitesettings.com
Corsair	Consider upgrading your keyboard and mouse to one that's designed specifically for gaming. Corsair is one of several companies that manufactures keyboards, mice, and headsets specifically for gamers.	www.corsair.com
Discord's *Fortnite* Forum	Visit this popular, online-based discussion group that has almost 400,000 members.	https://discordapp.com/invite/fortnite
Epic Game's Official Social Media Accounts for *Fortnite*	Visit the official Facebook, Twitter, and Instagram Accounts for *Fortnite*. Be sure to use the **#Fortnite** hashtag to find specific Twitter discussions and Instagram posts covering the game.	Facebook: www.facebook.com/FortniteGame Twitter: https://twitter.com/fortnitegame Instagram: www.instagram.com/fortnite
Fandom's *Fortnite* Wiki	Discover the latest news and strategies related to *Fortnite*.	http://fortnite.wikia.com/wiki/Fortnite_Wiki
FBR Insider	The *Fortnite: Battle Royale Insider* website offers game-related news, tips, and strategy videos.	www.fortniteinsider.com

WEBSITE OR YOUTUBE CHANNEL NAME	DESCRIPTION	URL
Fortnite Creative HQ	An independent online resource that showcases more than 3,000 Creative maps. Check out the Featured and Trending sections of the website to discover the very best maps.	www.fortnitecreativehq.com
Fortnite Gamepedia Wiki	Read up-to-date descriptions of every weapon, loot item, and ammo type available within *Fortnite.* This wiki also maintains a comprehensive database of soldier Outfits and related items released by Epic Games.	https://fortnite.gamepedia.com/Fortnite_Wiki For Mission-related information, visit: https://fortnite.gamepedia.com/Missions
Fortnite Scout	Check your personal player stats, and analyze your performance using a bunch of colorful graphs and charts. Also check out the stats of other *Fortnite: Battle Royale* players.	www.fortnitescout.com
Fortnite Skins	This independent website maintains a detailed database of all *Fortnite: Battle Royale* outfits and accessory items released by Epic Games.	https://fortniteskins.net
Fortnite Tracker Network	A website that showcases many Creative Maps and provides gamers with the codes to access them.	https://fortnitetracker.com/creative
Fortnite Weapon Stats & Info	This website offers up-to-date information on all of the weapons currently available in *Fortnite: Battle Royale.*	https://fortnitestats.com/weapons
Fortnite: Battle Royale for Android Mobile Devices	Download *Fortnite: Battle Royale* for your compatible Android-based mobile device.	www.epicgames.com/fortnite/en-US/mobile/android/get-started
Fortnite: Battle Royale Mobile (iOS App Store)	Download *Fortnite: Battle Royale* for your Apple iPhone or iPad	https://itunes.apple.com/us/app/fortnite/id1261357853

WEBSITE OR YOUTUBE CHANNEL NAME	DESCRIPTION	URL
Game Informer Magazine's *Fortnite* Coverage	Discover articles, reviews, and news about *Fortnite* published by *Game Informer* magazine.	www.gameinformer.com/fortnite
Gamepedia *Fortnite* Wiki	This website offers up-to-date information about all of the weapons, items, Outfits, etc., that are currently available in *Fortnite: Battle Royale.*	https://fortnite.gamepedia.com/Fortnite_Wiki
GameSpot's *Fortnite* Coverage	Check out the news, reviews, and game coverage related to *Fortnite* that's been published by GameSpot.	www.gamespot.com/fortnite
HyperX Gaming	Manufactures a selection of high-quality gaming keyboards, mice, headsets, and other accessories used by amateur and pro gamers alike. These work on PCs, Macs, and most console-based gaming systems.	www.hyperxgaming.com
IGN *Fortnite* Wiki Guide	Check out all IGN's past and current coverage of *Fortnite*.	www.ign.com/wikis/fortnite
Jason R. Rich's Websites and Social Media	Learn about additional, unofficial game strategy guides by Jason R. Rich that cover *Fortnite: Battle Royale*, *PUBG*, *Brawl Stars,* and *Apex Legends* (each sold separately).	www.JasonRich.com www.GameTipBooks.com Twitter: @JasonRich7 Instagram: @JasonRich7
Kyle Giersdorf (also known as "Bugha")	Winner of the 2019 *Fortnite* World Cup	YouTube: www. youtube.com/channel/ UCgIoEgOk3wzhhORNC9AbzhQ Twitch.tv: www.twitch.tv/bugha
LazarBeam	With more than 12 million subscribers, LazarBeam offers *Fortnite* tutorials that are not only informative, but very funny and extremely entertaining. You'll definitely want to subscribe to his YouTube channel!	YouTube Channel: http://goo.gl/HXwElg Twitter: https://twitter.com/LazarBeamYT Instagram: www.instagram.com/lazarbeamyt

WEBSITE OR YOUTUBE CHANNEL NAME	DESCRIPTION	URL
Microsoft's Xbox One *Fortnite* Website	Learn about and acquire *Fortnite: Battle Royale* if you're an Xbox One gamer.	www.microsoft.com/en-US/ store/p/Fortnite-Battle-Royalee/ BT5P2X999VH2
Ninja	Check out the live and recorded game streams from Ninja, one of the most highly skilled *Fortnite: Battle Royale* players in the world. His YouTube channel, for example, has more than 22 million subscribers.	YouTube: www.youtube.com/user/ NinjasHyper Mixer: www.mixer.com/ninja
Official Epic Games YouTube Channel for *Fortnite: Battle Royale*	The official *Fortnite: Battle Royale* YouTube channel.	www.youtube.com/user/epicfortnite
Razer	A company that offers high-end gaming controllers, keyboards, mice, and gaming headsets designed for more advanced gamers.	www.razer.com
Reddit's *Fortnite: Creative* Forum	Join thousands of *Fortnite* enthusiasts in an ongoing discussion that includes gaming tips and strategies.	www.reddit.com/r/Fortnite www.reddit.com/r/FortNiteBR
SCUF Gaming	This company makes high-end, extremely precise, customizable wireless controllers for console-based gaming systems, including the SCUF Impact controller for the PS4. If you're looking to enhance your reaction times when playing *Fortnite*, consider upgrading your wireless controller.	www.scufgaming.com
Turtle Beach Corp.	This is one of many companies that make great quality, wired or wireless (Bluetooth) gaming headsets that work with all gaming platforms.	www.turtlebeach.com

New Missions and More Challenges Are Always on the Way!

The addition of Missions and Challenges to *Fortnite: Battle Royale* gives gamers yet another fun and challenging way to experience the game in Solo, Duos, Squads, or one of the limited-time game play modes (such as Team Rumble). Missions and Challenges are not offered in Creative or Playground mode.

As you'll discover, there are two approaches you can take to complete the Missions and Challenges. During matches, you can focus on achieving #1 Battle Royale, engage in combat, and engage in all of the tasks required to stay alive and achieve victory, while also trying to complete one or more Challenges per match.

An easier option is to focus just on completing Missions and Challenges to receive Battle Stars, while at the same time, avoiding as much enemy confrontation as possible during matches. In this case, winning matches and achieving #1 Victory Royale is not a priority! (As you learned, this is often even easier if you participate in Team Rumble matches and earn Battle Stars, as opposed to Solo, Duos, or Squads matches.)

Since you're able to work on multiple Challenges at once during a single match, if you focus on the specific objectives that need to be accomplished, it's sometimes possible to receive 20 or more Battle Stars during a single match. This is enough Battle Stars to unlock at least two Battle Pass Tiers.

Unlocking Battle Pass Tiers, and completing other Missions and Challenges offered when playing Fortnite: Battle Royale *will help you become a better, more well-rounded gamer over time, since individual Challenges require you to focus on and use specific gaming skills and you continuously become better acquainted with the island, as well as the vehicles, weapons, items, tools, and resources that are typically available to you during a match.*

While you're becoming a better gamer over time by completing Missions and Challenges, and by unlocking Battle Pass Tiers, you'll also expand your soldier's Locker with exclusive Outfits, Emotes, and related items, without having to spend a lot of extra money on purchases from the Item Shop.

Let's Do Some Number Crunching

Between all of the Outfits, Emotes, and items offered as Rewards for unlocking the 100 Tiers associated with a Battle Pass, you'll quickly discover that the money you spend acquiring a Battle Pass each season is well worth the investment.

For example, you'll typically need to spend 950 V-Bucks (about $9.50 US) to purchase a Battle Pass each season. The Reward for unlocking various Tiers is sometimes a bundle of 100 V-Bucks.

During Season 10, for example, if you unlocked all 100 Tiers related to just the Battle Pass, you'd receive a total of 1,500 V-Bucks (15 separate 100 V-Buck bundles), not to mention thousands of V-Bucks worth of exclusive Outfits, Emotes, and related items.

Unlocking Tier 100 of a Battle Pass guarantees that you'll unlock an ultra-exclusive, Legendary Outfit, such as Ultima Knight, which was the final Reward for completing Season 10's Battle Pass.

Add to this all of the extra Rewards associated with completing Event and Style-related Challenges, as well as Free Pass Challenges, and the time you spend completing Missions and Challenges is definitely a worthwhile (not to mention fun and challenging) investment.

Expect Something New Each Week

Every week, Epic Games releases new Missions and Challenges within *Fortnite: Battle Royale*. Plus, as you complete Challenges during most Missions, additional Challenges and Prestige Challenges get unlocked.

As a result, in addition to everything new that's added to the game as part of the weekly game updates and more extensive season-related updates (such as new points of interest on the map, new weapons, new vehicles, new Health/Shield replenishment items, new tools, and new types of terrain), you can always experience the latest Missions and Challenges that are virtually guaranteed to keep you from getting bored!

Most importantly, as you now know, participating in Missions and Challenges will help you become a better *Fortnite: Battle Royale* gamer, because each Challenge will force you to practice one or more of the core skills and responsibilities required to achieve #1 Victory Royale (such as combat, exploration, resource gathering, arsenal management, driving vehicles, avoiding the storm, and basic survival).

Final Thoughts . . .

As always, when playing *Fortnite: Battle Royale*, have fun! Also, if you're able to do it, enjoy the bragging rights associated with showcasing the ultra-exclusive Outfit that's the reward for unlocking Battle Pass Tier 100 each gaming season! Filling up your soldier's Locker with the most exclusive Outfits and related items will definitely make your gaming friends jealous and help you prove that you're a gamer not to be messed with.

To learn about other unofficial *Fortnite* strategy guides which are part of this incredibly popular *Master Combat* series, be sure to visit: **www.FortniteGameBooks.com** and to follow author Jason R. Rich on Instagram, Twitter, and Facebook at @JasonRich7.

ALSO AVAILABLE!

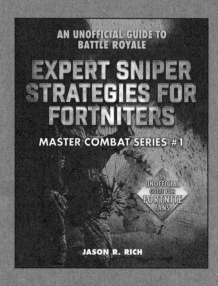

AN UNOFFICIAL GUIDE TO BATTLE ROYALE

EXPERT SNIPER STRATEGIES FOR FORTNITERS

MASTER COMBAT SERIES #1

JASON R. RICH

AN UNOFFICIAL GUIDE TO BATTLE ROYALE

EXPERT SECRETS TO ISLAND TRAVEL FOR FORTNITERS

MASTER COMBAT SERIES #2

JASON R. RICH

AN UNOFFICIAL GUIDE TO BATTLE ROYALE

ALL-TERRAIN SURVIVAL FOR FORTNITERS

MASTER COMBAT SERIES #3

JASON R. RICH

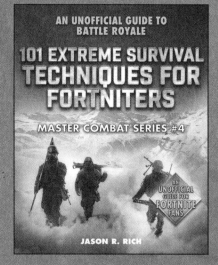

AN UNOFFICIAL GUIDE TO BATTLE ROYALE

101 EXTREME SURVIVAL TECHNIQUES FOR FORTNITERS

MASTER COMBAT SERIES #4

JASON R. RICH

AN UNOFFICIAL GUIDE TO BATTLE ROYALE

CREATIVE EXPERT FOR FORTNITERS

MASTER COMBAT SERIES #5

JASON R. RICH

**Sky Pony Press
New York**